Mental Health in Learning Disabilities

A reader

Third edition

Edited by: Geraldine Holt, Steve Hardy and Nick Bouras

Pavilion

estia centre

Mental Health in Learning Disabilities
A reader

Published by:
Pavilion Publishing (Brighton) Ltd
Richmond House
Richmond Road
Brighton BN2 3RL
Tel: 01273 623222
Fax: 01273 625526
Email: info@pavpub.com
Web: www.pavpub.com

First published 2005. Reprinted 2006.

A Catalogue record for this book is available from the British Library.

ISBN-13: 978 1 84196 172 9
ISBN-10: 1 84196 173 6

Pavilion is the leading training and development provider and publisher in the health, social care and allied fields, providing a range of innovative training solutions underpinned by sound research and professional values. We aim to put our customers first, through excellent customer service and good value.

Editor: Grace Fairley
Cover design: Tony Pitt
Page layout: Jigsaw Design
Printing: Ashford Press (Southampton)

Contents

Introduction

This reader, like its previous editions in 1995 and 1997, aims to provide the reader with up-to-date information on mental health problems in people with learning disabilities, and associated issues.

Since the previous editions, we have seen many changes in the field of mental health and services for people with learning disabilities. Community services are now well established, and the involvement of service users in all aspects of health and social care is of primary importance. We have seen the implementation of the National Service Framework for Mental Health (DH, 1999) setting standards for the delivery of care. Over the last five years, the four countries of the United Kingdom have produced new policies on meeting the needs of people with learning disabilities, signalling new agendas for services. This has included supporting people to access mainstream services and a changing role for specialist learning disability services and the confirmation that the Care Programme Approach is applicable to people with learning disabilities who have mental problems. The use of psychological therapies for people with learning disabilities has gained growing recognition, and services are seeing an increase in rate of referrals for offending behaviour.

With this in mind, this reader is a completely new edition. All previous chapters have been rewritten and six new chapters have been added, including working with families, offenders with learning disabilities, cultural diversity, psychological and social interventions.

Contributors are from a multidisciplinary background and include psychiatrists, psychologists, social workers, family therapists, nurses and trainers. All are experts in delivering mental health services to people with learning disabilities, and have an interest in staff training.

The chapters of this reader provide background reading for facilitators of *Mental Health in Learning Disabilities: A training resource*. Nonetheless, participants from the training workshops, as well as professionals who would like a basic knowledge of mental health problems and people with learning disabilities, will find much to interest and inform them.

We would like to thank all the contributors to this reader, and especially Peter Woodward for his assistance during the editorial process.

Geraldine Holt, Steve Hardy and Nick Bouras

About the editors

Geraldine Holt BSc (Hons), FRCPsych is consultant psychiatrist at South London and Maudsley NHS Trust, and honorary senior lecturer at the Institute of Psychiatry, King's College London. She was previously senior policy adviser on learning disabilities at the Department of Health. She has published widely on the mental health of people with learning disabilities. She serves on a number of national and international bodies with this focus.

Steve Hardy RNLD, MSc is training and consultancy manager at the Estia Centre, South London and Maudsley NHS Trust. He is a member of the Royal College of Nursing Steering Committee on Learning Disability and founder/co-ordinator of the Mental Health in Learning Disabilities Network. He has worked in mental health services for people with learning disabilities for the past 11 years and has published several articles in this area. His interests include mental health promotion, service user involvement and staff training. Steve is also a citizen advocate.

Nick Bouras MD, PhD, FRCPsych is professor of psychiatry at the Institute of Psychiatry, King's College London and consultant psychiatrist at South London and the Maudsley NHS Trust. He has been an executive member of several national and international organisations including the World Psychiatric Association, European Association MH–MR and International Association for the Scientific Study of Intellectual Disability. He has published extensively on community psychiatry and mental health aspects for people with learning disabilities and he has edited several books.

Contributors

Jane Barnes CQSW, ASW
Senior Social Worker, ASW, Accredited
Practice Teacher and Lecturer
London Borough of Southwark
Monks Orchard House
Bethlem Royal Hospital
Monks Orchard Road
Beckenham
Kent BR3 3BX

Peter Carpenter MB, ChB, BSc, FRCPsych
Consultant Psychiatrist in Learning
Disability and Honorary Senior Lecturer
Bath & North East Somerset Primary
Care Trust and University of Bristol
Kingswood Learning Disability Service
Hanham Road
Kingswood
Bristol BS15 8PQ

Helen Costello PhD, MSc, BA Joint
Honours
Research Co-ordinator
South London and Maudsley NHS Trust
Estia Centre
66 Snowsfields
London SE1 3SS

Karen Dodd BSc, PhD, MSc, AFBPS
Head of Psychology
Surrey Oaklands NHS Trust
Ramsey House
West Park, Horton Lane
Epsom
Surrey KT19 8PB

Andrew Flynn BA, MRCPsych
Consultant Psychiatrist – Mental
Health in Learning Disabilities
Oxleas NHS Trust
183 Lodge Hill
Goldie Leigh
London SE2 0AY

Dan Geer MSc
Behaviour Support Specialist
South London and Maudsley
NHS Trust
Southwark Community Team for
Adults with Learning Disabilities
121 Townley Road
London SE22 8SW

Shaun Gravestock MBBS, MRCPsych
Consultant Psychiatrist in Adult
Mental Health of Learning Disability
and Honorary Senior Lecturer
Oxleas NHS Trust and Estia Centre
Greenwich Community Learning
Disability Team
Civic House
20 Grand Depot Road
London SE18 6SJ

Richard Hammond RNLD, BSc
(Hons)
Ward Manager
South London and Maudsley
NHS Trust
York Clinic
Guy's Hospital
47 Weston Street
London SE1 3RR

Colin Hemmings BSc, MB BS, MSc,
MRCPsych
Locum Consultant Psychiatrist in
Learning Disabilities
South London and Maudsley
NHS Trust
Department of Mental Health in
Learning Disabilities
York Clinic
Guy's Hospital
47 Weston Street
London SE1 3RR

Jayne Henry BSc (Hons), DClinPsy.
Clinical Psychologist
Hertfordshire Partnership NHS Trust
Warren Court
Eric Shepherd Unit
Woodside Road
Abbots Langley
Hertfordshire WD5 0HT

Stephen Higgins MSc, RMN, RNLD
Senior Tutor
Estia Centre and the Institute of
Psychiatry
66 Snowsfields
London SE1 3SS

Geraldine Holt
Consultant Psychiatrist
Estia Centre
66 Snowsfields
London SE1 3SS

Natalie Hiser D. Clin. Psych
Clinical Psychologist
Oxleas NHS Trust
Bracton Centre
Bracton Lane
Leyton Cross Road
Dartford DA2 7AP

Chris Hodgkins BSc (Hons)
Trainee Clinical Psychologist
University of Leicester
University Road
Leicester LE1 7RH

Theresa Joyce BSc, MSc, Ph.D.,
AFBPS, C.Psychol.
Head of Psychology, Services for
Adults with Learning Disabilities
South London and Maudsley
NHS Trust
Estia Centre
66 Snowsfields
London SE1 3SS

Jim Molloy Dip. Applied Psychology
of Challenging Behaviour
Team Co-ordinator (Psychology and
Behaviour Support Team)
South London and Maudsley
NHS Trust
Southwark Community Team for
Adults with Learning Disabilities
121 Townley Road
London SE22 8SW

Gervase Newrick
Behaviour Support Specialist
South London and Maudsley
NHS Trust
Southwark Community Team for
Adults with Learning Disabilities
121 Townley Road
London SE22 8SW

Jean O'Hara MBBS MRCPsych
Consultant Psychiatrist – Mental
Health in Learning Disabilities
South London and Maudsley NHS
Trust and the Estia Centre
York Clinic
Guy's Hospital
47 Weston Street
London SE1 3RR

Barley Oliver BSc, D. Clin. Psych.
Consultant Clinical Psychologist
South London and Maudsley
NHS Trust
Lewisham Community Team for
Adults with Learning Disabilities
19–21 Brownhill Road
London SE6 2HG

Carol Paton BSc, DipClinPharm,
MRPharmS, MCMHP
Chief Pharmacist
Oxleas NHS Trust
Pharmacy
Pinewood House
Pinewood Place
Dartford, Kent DA2 7WG

Helen Philp BSc, MSc
Family Therapist
South London and Maudsley
NHS Trust
Monks Orchard House
Bethlem Royal Hospital
Monks Orchard Road
Beckenham
Kent BR3 3BX

Max Pickard MB BS, BSc,
MRCPsych
Specialist Registrar
South London and Maudsley
NHS Trust
Department of Mental Health in
Learning Disabilities
York Clinic
Guy's Hospital
47 Weston Street
London SE1 3RR

Raghu Raghavan BA, MSc, RNLD,
PGCE, PhD
Senior Lecturer
University of Bradford
School of Health Studies
Unity Building
Trinity Road
Bradford
West Yorkshire BD5 0BB

David Rose BA (Hons) MA, Dip SW,
ClinPsyD
Clinical Psychologist
Dudley South NHS Primary Care
Trust
Psychology Services
Shousters House
Ridge Hill, Brierley Hill Road
Stourbridge DY8 5ST

John Rose, BSc, MSc, M. Clin. Psy.,
PhD.
Lecturer and Consultant Clinical
Psychologist
Dudley South Primary Care Trust
& The University of Birmingham
The School of Psychology
The University of Birmingham
Edgbaston
Birmingham B15 2TT

Penny Smith BSc, MSc, CPSychol
Clinical Team Co-ordinator
(Psychology) and Counselling
Psychologist
South London and Maudsley
NHS Trust
Lambeth Community for Adults
with Learning Disabilities
340 Brixton Road
London SW9 7AA

The Tuesday Group
C/O Lewisham Mencap
72 Lee High Road
London SE13 5PT

Jeremy Turk MD, BSc (Hons),
FRCPsych, FRCPCH, DCH
Reader in Developmental Psychiatry
St. George's Hospital Medical School,
University of London
Department of Clinical
Developmental Sciences
Jenner Wing
St. George's Hospital Medical School
Cranmer Terrace
London SW17 0RE

Vicky Turk BSc, MSc, PhD, AsFBPS
Consultant Clinical Psychologist
Oxleas NHS Trust
Erith Centre
Park Crescent
Erith
Kent DA8 3EE

Robert Winterhalder MRCPsych
Consultant Psychiatrist and Senior
Fellow
Bromley Primary Care Trust and
Estia Centre
Bassetts Centre
Starts Hill Road
Farnborough
Orpington
Kent BR6 7WF

Peter Woodward RNLD, MSc, Dip.
Applied Psychology, Dip. HENS
Training Officer
South London and Maudsley NHS
Trust
Estia Centre
66 Snowsfields
London SE1 3SS

Kiriakos Xenitidis MSc, MRCPsych,
MD
Consultant Psychiatrist and Honorary
Senior Lecturer
South London and Maudsley NHS
Trust and the Institute of Psychiatry
Monks Orchard House
Bethlem Royal Hospital
Monks Orchard Road
Beckenham
Kent BR3 3BX

CHAPTER ONE

Psychiatric disorders in adults with learning disabilities

SHAUN GRAVESTOCK, ANDREW FLYNN AND COLIN HEMMINGS

Introduction

The term 'psychiatric disorders' is used broadly here to include psychiatric illness, personality disorder and challenging behaviour requiring specialist psychiatric assessment and management. Adults with learning disabilities who also have such psychiatric disorders usually require focussed and evidence based specialist clinical and service responses (Deb *et al*, 2001).

This chapter focuses on adults with learning disabilities who have psychiatric disorders. Later chapters more specifically address the issues for other groups of people with learning disabilities who have psychiatric disorders, including autism, older adults, children and offenders (see Chapters 12, 13, 14 and 16).

This chapter covers the causes, presentations and types of psychiatric illness, personality disorder and challenging behaviour. Understanding of these issues should allow learning disabilities and mental health services staff to work in partnership to assess and better meet the mental health needs of adults with learning disabilities (Vanstraelen, Holt & Bouras, 2003).

What is a psychiatric disorder?

Adults with learning disabilities often experience psychological or emotional distress after stressful life events. Their emotional, psychological, functional and behavioural responses can be seen as understandable and perhaps even adaptive or restorative. However, occasionally these responses are especially intense, traumatic, disturbing and maladaptive, resulting in serious disruption to the lives of the person and others.

An adult with learning disabilities exhibiting disturbed mental state and behaviour, causing distress to themselves or others, can then be considered to have a psychiatric disorder. Sometimes other terms are used such as 'mental disorder', 'mental health problem' or 'mental health needs' (Deb *et al*, 2001, Royal College of Psychiatrists, 2001).

Terminology: psychiatric disorder, challenging behaviour, autism and behavioural phenotypes

The concept of psychiatric disorder in adults with learning disabilities is broader than that of challenging behaviour per se. The mental health assessment aims to consider a broad range of internal experiences (mood, thoughts, beliefs, perceptions, memories etc) as well as externally exhibited behavioural and social functioning issues. However, the concept of challenging behaviour does usefully focus attention on the interaction between individuals with learning disabilities and their social, physical and service environments. To avoid later confusions, the terms 'challenging behaviour', 'autism' and 'behavioural phenotypes' will be explained at this point (Vanstraelen, Holt & Bouras, 2003).

Challenging behaviour refers to severe and usually chronic combinations of aggressive, destructive, attention-seeking, sexually inappropriate, self-injurious, noisy, hyperactive, and socially inappropriate (for example, stereotypies, faecal smearing or running-away) behaviours (see Chapter 7). Challenging behaviour occurs in 20–40% of adults with learning disabilities, and severe challenging behaviour occurs in 5–6%. Severe and chronic challenging behaviour presents challenges for service providers as they threaten the physical safety of the adult with learning disabilities and others, and the adult with learning disabilities risks exclusion from mainstream services (Emerson, Moss & Kiernan, 1999).

The disturbed mental states of adults with learning disabilities with psychiatric disorders do often present with challenging behaviour, including sometimes life-threatening behaviours towards themselves or others. Some challenging behaviours might be signs or symptoms of an underlying psychiatric illness (Vanstraelen, Holt & Bouras 2003).

For example, being very irritable and overactive are symptoms of the affective disorder mania. Severe anxiety can present with aggression. Repeated overdoses or wrist cutting are symptoms of borderline personality disorder. However, not all adults with psychiatric disorders exhibit challenging behaviour. For example, some adults with learning disabilities suffering with depression put on a 'brave face', hide how they are feeling and struggle to maintain their functioning.

Further, not all challenging behaviour is due to underlying psychiatric disorders. The developmental level of the adult with learning disabilities also needs to be considered. Many adults with severe learning disabilities and some with autism lack the communication skills to say they are feeling physically unwell or are unhappy for perfectly understandable reasons. Thus, adults with severe learning disabilities and those with autism may exhibit challenging behaviour to communicate that they are unhappy or feeling physically unwell (Emerson, Moss & Kiernan, 1999) (see Chapters 7 and 12).

Behavioural phenotypes are repertoires of maladaptive and adaptive behaviours characteristically associated with specific genetic conditions causing learning disabilities. Examples include:

- Fragile-X syndrome is associated with learning disabilities, physical anomalies, speech problems, hyperactivity and autistic-like features

- Down syndrome is associated with learning disabilities, physical anomalies, obsessive, stubborn and avoiding behaviours and an increased risk of Alzheimer's dementia

- Prader-Willi syndrome is associated with learning disabilities, physical anomalies, insatiable appetite, gross overeating, obesity, skin-picking, irritability and stubbornness (Berney, 2003).

Causes of psychiatric disorders

Adults with learning disabilities are at increased risk of developing psychiatric disorders due to the complex interaction of often multiple biological, psychological, social and family factors (Deb *et al*, 2001; Royal College of Psychiatrists, 2001). The important vulnerability factors to be considered during psychiatric assessment are listed in **Table 1.1** overleaf. (See also Chapters 2 and 13 for further discussion of how these factors impact on the assessment of adults with learning disabilities.)

Table 1.1: Vulnerability factors for psychiatric disorders		
Biological	1	Brain damage/epilepsy
	2	Vision/hearing impairments
	3	Physical illnesses/disabilities
	4	Genetic/familial conditions (autism, behavioural phenotypes etc)
	5	Drugs/alcohol abuse
	6	Medication/physical treatments
Psychological	7	Rejection/deprivation/abuse
	8	Life events/separations/losses
	9	Poor problem solving/coping strategies
	10	Social/emotional/sexual vulnerabilities
	11	Poor self-acceptance/low self-esteem
	12	Devaluation/disempowerment
Family	13	Diagnostic/bereavement issues
	14	Life-cycle transitions/crises
	15	Stress/adaptation to disability
	16	Limited social/community networks
	17	Difficulties 'letting go'
Social	18	Negative attitudes/expectations
	19	Stigmatisation/prejudice/social exclusion
	20	Poor supports/relationships/networks
	21	Inappropriate environments/services
	22	Financial/legal disadvantages

People unaccustomed to working with adults with learning disabilities may exhibit the phenomenon of 'diagnostic overshadowing'. This occurs when clear signs of a psychiatric disorder are inappropriately attributed to a person's learning disabilities per se, and are not seen as resulting from mental health needs. Alternatively, individuals may be misdiagnosed as having a psychotic illness when their developmental level has not been fully considered as an explanation for the primitive behaviours, reduced social functioning, and disorganised thoughts and speech which may accompany periods of stress, confusion and change for adults with learning disabilities (Deb *et al*, 2001, Royal College of Psychiatrists, 2001).

Presentations of psychiatric disorders

The presentation of a psychiatric disorder in an adult with learning disabilities will depend on their usual developmental level, ie their usual levels of cognitive, communicative, physical and social functioning, and behavioural repertoire. The presentation will also be determined by the past and present interpersonal, cultural and environmental influences for that individual (Deb *et al*, 2001; Royal College of Psychiatrists, 2001; Vanstraelen, Holt & Bouras, 2003).

Generally, the signs and symptoms of psychiatric disorders presented by adults with mild learning disabilities and reasonable verbal communication skills are similar but less complex than those presented by adults of average intellect. However, adults with moderate–severe learning disabilities, and those with autism, have less well-developed cognitive and communication skills, as well as increased risks of physical impairments. Thus, they are more likely to exhibit disturbed and regressed behaviours and biological functions, and possible physical ill-health signs, as presentations of psychiatric disorders (see **Table 1.2**).

Table 1.2 Presentations of psychiatric disorders in adults with mild and severe learning disabilities as compared to those in adults of average intellect		
Psychiatric disorder	**Presentation in mild learning disabilities**	**Presentation in severe learning disabilities**
Dementias	Similar	Different/difficult to diagnose
Acute confusion (delirium)	Similar/underdiagnosed	Similar/difficult to diagnose
Schizophrenic psychoses	Similar/may be overdiagnosed	Very different/difficult to diagnose
Affective psychoses	Similar/underdiagnosed	Different/underdiagnosed
Anxiety and related disorders	Similar/underdiagnosed	Very different/difficult to diagnose
Eating disorders	Similar/underdiagnosed	Different/difficult to diagnose
Personality disorders	Similar	Different/difficult to diagnose

As shown in **Table 1.2**, some psychiatric disorders can be difficult to accurately diagnose. Generally speaking, it is more difficult to diagnose the more complex psychiatric disorders such as dementia and psychosis, especially in adults with severe learning disabilities. Further, an individual may present with overlapping signs and symptoms of two or more related psychiatric disorders at a given time, as the clinical examples below illustrate:

- A man with mild learning disabilities and epilepsy presented with long-standing excessive attention to his personal hygiene due to an obsessional personality disorder, together with recent panic attacks and hyperventilation due to an anxiety disorder.

- A middle-aged woman with Down syndrome and moderate learning disabilities presented with a recent onset of low mood, disturbed sleep and appetite due to a depressive disorder, set against a background of gradually declining social and self-care skills, due to Alzheimer's dementia.

- A teenager with severe learning disabilities, no speech, social indifference, fear of water and finger-flicking since childhood, due to autism, presented with self-injurious and sexually inappropriate challenging behaviours following changes in his daytime activities programme.

- A woman with moderate learning disabilities due to Prader-Willi syndrome has longstanding overeating and self-injurious skin picking, ie the characteristic behavioural phenotype. She became depressed following her mother's death and presented with social withdrawal, sleep disturbance, binge eating episodes and food pica (eating food out of rubbish bins).

Types of psychiatric disorder

Adults with learning disabilities suffer from the same types of psychiatric disorders as people of average intellect. However, the causes and presentations of psychiatric disorders are determined by the vulnerability factors and developmental level of the individual, as discussed above. For example, psychoses are difficult to diagnose when individuals are unable to verbalise complex distressing experiences such as odd ideas and hearing voices. The diagnosis of dementia and personality disorders may be difficult in adults with learning disabilities, as it is hard to obtain an accurate baseline and long-term account of functioning, behaviours and symptoms (Deb *et al*, 2001; Royal College of Psychiatrists, 2001).

Schizophrenia spectrum disorders

The presentation of psychoses in verbally proficient people with mild learning disabilities are similar to those seen in people without learning disabilities. However, people with learning disabilities who have schizophrenia have a tendency to show less psychopathology (such as persecutory delusions and formal thought disorder) and increased displays of bizarre behaviour. The content of delusions tends to be more bland and unremarkable, on account of the reduced social opportunities open to people with learning disabilities. For example, someone of average intellect may believe they are embroiled in a spy scenario and that the secret service are plotting against them, whereas someone with learning disabilities may believe that people are talking about them. As the severity of learning disability increases, paranoid symptoms and catatonia can become more prominent (Meadows *et al*, 1991; Tyrer & Dunstan, 1997). It is very difficult to diagnose schizophrenia in people with severe learning disabilities, due to their limited verbal skills.

These disorders can be over-diagnosed in adults with learning disabilities who may exhibit stress-related confusion, odd behaviours, muddled speech and suspiciousness. It is often difficult to be certain whether hallucinations are being experienced by an adult with learning disabilities (Deb *et al*, 2001; Royal College of Psychiatrists, 2001).

Organic psychotic disorders

Acute confusion (delirium) caused by constipation, medication, infections, or epilepsy may not be noticed. It usually resolves with treatment of the underlying physical causes. Repeated and prolonged acute confusional episodes may herald the progressive deterioration seen in dementia (see Chapter 13).

Delirium in people with learning disabilities is characterised by clouding of consciousness, particularly at night, disorientation, impairment of memory, illusions, visual hallucinations and fearfulness (Wilson, 1997). Visual hallucinations are more characteristic of organic psychosis (eg drug induced, seizure activity-related) than non-organic psychosis.

As adults with learning disabilities live longer, dementia is increasingly diagnosed. Ageing adults with Down syndrome have an increased risk of developing dementia, especially Alzheimer's dementia. Roughly 8% of adults with Down syndrome aged 35–50 years and 65% of those aged over 60 develop Alzheimer's dementia. They may present with loss of skills, social withdrawal, behaviour problems, epilepsy, depression or incontinence. Reduced functioning in ageing adults with Down syndrome may also be due to their increased risk of developing a hearing loss, cataracts, depression and thyroid underactivity (see Chapter 13).

Affective psychotic disorders

Affective psychoses often run in families and can present as cyclical manic, depressive or mixed disorders. Disturbed activity levels and biological and social functioning often accompany irritability in mania, and bodily complaints in depression. Regression, confusion, vomiting, and self-injurious and aggressive behaviours may also be symptoms and signs of affective disorders (Vanstraelen, Holt & Bouras, 2003).

Depression

The psychopathology of depressive disorders in people with mild learning disabilities is similar to that demonstrated by those without learning disabilities, although some may present atypically, for example with weight gain rather than the typical weight loss or hypersomnia rather than the typical difficulty in sleeping. The onset of depression in people with learning disabilities tends to be more insidious and changes seen tend to be less dramatic (Deb *et al*, 2001; Ballinger, 1997). Some symptoms have an increased prominence in people with mild learning disabilities, such as loss of confidence, increases in tearfulness and deterioration in social and self help skills (Marston, Perry & Roy, 1997; Helsel and Matson, 1988). Psychotic symptoms such as delusions of guilt or hypochondria may occur, but tend to be less complex than in those without learning disabilities.

The presentation of depression changes as the person's learning disabilities become more severe. Increased dependence, psychomotor agitation, irritability, stereotypies, screaming and a worsening of existing behavioural problems such as self–injurious behaviour and temper tantrums have been described in people with more severe learning disabilities (Meins, 1995; Reiss & Rojahn, 1993).

Bipolar affective disorder

In bipolar affective disorder, a person has episodes of depression and mania. Mania may be recognised by an increase in motor activity, rises in intrusive and destructive behaviour, assaults and self–abuse. There maybe evidence of pressure of speech and, less commonly, flight of ideas (Wilson, 1997; Hassan & Mooney, 1979). In hypomania, verbal symptoms such as flight of ideas are rare. Grandiose delusions may be expressed, but in more simple forms than those of average intellect (Ballinger, 1997). For example, someone of average intellect may believe they are the Queen, and expect to be treated as such, where as someone with learning disabilities may believe that they are an electrician. Rapid cycling bipolar disorder is when a person experiences more than four episodes of either mania or depression in a year. It is believed that this disorder is more common among people with learning disabilities (Vanstraelen & Tyrer, 1999).

Anxiety and related disorders

Reactive depression commonly follows life events such as the loss of a significant carer, friend or pet, or placement changes, but may not be recognised. Anxiety states may also develop in response to stress and environmental changes. Generalised anxiety may present with agitation, panic attacks, low mood, non–epileptic attacks, physical health concerns and over-demanding behaviours (Deb *et al*, 2001; Royal College of Psychiatrists, 2001). Common symptoms of anxiety disorders in people with learning disabilities are identifiable as overactivity, agoraphobia, sexual dysfunction, mood changes, depersonalisation and derealisiation, somatic complaints, sleep and appetite disturbances (Stavrakaki & Mintsioulis, 1997).

Phobias tend to be over-diagnosed when a refusal to try something new may represent more general avoidance of possible failure. However, specific phobias, for example, of dogs, dirt, water, heights or falling may occur, particularly in adults with autism. The repetitive thoughts, ritualistic and obsessive behaviours which are resisted and cause anxiety to those with obsessive-compulsive disorder may be misdiagnosed as features of autism (Deb *et al*, 2001; Royal College of Psychiatrists, 2001).

Eating disorders

Adults with mild–severe learning disabilities can present with binge eating disorders and associated overweight or obesity. Pica (eating inedible substances) and food regurgitation/rumination with significant underweight are most likely to occur in adults with severe learning disabilities. Extreme food faddiness and refusal with significant underweight are often associated with eating/food related rituals and obsessions in those with autism. Less commonly, cases of anorexia nervosa and bulimia nervosa occur in adults with mild–moderate learning disabilities (Royal College of Psychiatrists, 2001; Deb *et al*, 2001).

Personality disorders

Adults with learning disabilities exhibit the full range of personality assets, difficulties and disorders. The diagnosis of personality disorders remains controversial, due to the overlap with other psychiatric disorders and challenging behaviours in adults with learning disabilities. However, chronic maladaptive patterns of behaviour and relating to others, which are not adequately explained by autism or other psychiatric disorders, may be best considered as due to a personality disorder. While personality disorders are more likely to be diagnosed in adults with mild and moderate learning disabilities, similar presentations in adults with severe learning disabilities are more likely to be seen as challenging behaviours (Deb *et al*, 2001; Royal College of Psychiatrists, 2001).

Conclusion

This chapter discussed the vulnerability factors, presentations and types of psychiatric disorders. As comprehensive local services evolve, psychiatrists have vital roles to play in sharing their skills with diverse staff and professional groups concerned with mental health issues. Knowledge about vulnerability factors can underpin evidence-based mental health promotion and prevention strategies (Deb *et al*, 2001). Understanding the presentations and types of psychiatric disorders will assist those supporting adults with learning disabilities to ensure timely access to appropriate mental health services. Then, co-ordinated, evidence-based clinical, supportive and social care inputs have the best chance to reduce the adverse effects of psychiatric disorders on the mental, physical and social well-being of adults with learning disabilities and their carers.

References and further reading

Ballinger CB (1997) Affective Disorders. In: S Read (Ed) *Psychiatry in Learning Disability*. London: Saunders.

Berney T (2003) Behavioural phenotypes. In: W Fraser and M Kerr (Eds) *Seminars in the psychiatry of learning disabilities*. Second Edition. London: Gaskell and Royal College of Psychiatrists.

Deb S, Matthews T, Holt G & Bouras N (2001) *Practice Guidelines for the Assessment and Diagnosis of Mental Health Problems in Adults with Intellectual Disability*. Brighton: Pavilion Publishing.

Emerson E, Moss S & Kiernan C (1999) The relationship between challenging behaviour and psychiatric disorders in people with severe developmental disabilities. In: N Bouras (Ed) *Psychiatric and Behavioural Disorders in Developmental Disabilities and Mental Retardation*. Cambridge: Cambridge University Press.

Gilberg C, Persson E, Grufman M & Themner U (1986) Psychiatric disorders in mildly and severely mentally retarded urban children and adolescents: Epidemiological aspects. *British Journal of Psychiatry* 149, 68–74.

Hassan MK & Mooney RP (1979) Three cases of manic depressive illness in mentally retarded adults. *American Journal of Psychiatry* 176, 32–36.

Helsel WJ & Matson JL (1988) The relationship of depression to social skills and intellectual functioning in mentally retarded adults. *Journal of Mental Deficiency Research* 32, 411–418.

Marston GM, Perry DW & Roy A (1997) Manifestations of depression in people with intellectual disability. *Journal of Intellectual Disability Research* 41, 476–480.

Meadows G, Turner T, Cambell L, Lewis SW, Reverley MA & Murray RM (1991) Assessing schizophrenia in adults with mental retardation: a comparative study. *British Journal of Psychiatry* 158, 103–105.

Meins W (1995) Symptoms of major depression in mentally retarded adults. *Journal of Intellectual Disability Research* 39, 41–45.

Reiss S & Rojahn J (1993) Joint occurrence of depression and in children and adults with mental retardation. *Journal of Intellectual Disability Research* 37, 287–294.

Royal College of Psychiatrists (2001) *DC-LD: Diagnostic Criteria for Psychiatric Disorders for use with Adults with Learning Disabilities/Mental Retardation.* London: Gaskell.

Stavrakaki C & Mintsioulis G (1997) Implications of clinical study of anxiety disorders in persons with mental retardation. *Psychiatric Annals* 27, 182–189.

Tyrer SP & Dunstan JA (1997) Schizophrenia. In: S Reed (Ed) *Psychiatry in Learning Disability.* London: Saunders.

Vanstraelen M, Holt G & Bouras N (2003) Adults with learning disabilities and psychiatric problems. In: W Fraser and M Kerr (Eds) *Seminars in the psychiatry of learning disabilities.* Second Edition. London: Gaskell and Royal College of Psychiatrists.

Vanstraelen M & Tryrer SP (1999) Rapid cycling bipolar affective disorder in people with intellectual disability: a systematic review. *Journal of Intellectual Disability Research* **43** (5) 349–359.

Wilson D (1997) Psychiatric disorders and mild learning disability. In: O Russell (Ed) *Seminars in the Psychiatry of Learning Disabilities.* London: Gaskell.

CHAPTER TWO

Assessment of mental health problems

STEVE HARDY AND GERALDINE HOLT

Introduction

Ensuring that people with learning disabilities get appropriate help for their mental health problems is not just the responsibility of health and social care professionals. Support staff and carers have an essential role in ensuring that mental health problems are identified and that service users are referred for comprehensive assessment. This chapter introduces some of the major issues in recognising and assessing mental health problems in people with learning disabilities.

Detecting mental health problems

In the general population, the first contact for someone who may have a mental health problem is often their general practitioner (GP). They or others may have noticed a change in their behaviour, feelings or thoughts, such as difficulty in sleeping, expressing feelings of sadness, having paranoid thoughts or a change in their ability to cope with everyday life. These may have been precipitated by a change in circumstance, such as a relationship breakdown or unemployment. The GP will assess if the person has a mental health problem and whether or not they need to be referred to a specialist mental health service.

For people with learning disabilities, the route to appropriate mental health care is often a difficult path. Firstly, it needs to be recognised that there is a change in the person's behaviour, feelings or thoughts, and that this may be due to a mental health problem. The person themselves may not realise that they have a problem, or may have difficulty in self-advocating and letting other know how they are feeling. The development of a mental health problem is often insidious, slowly developing over a period of time. It may be difficult for staff and carers to pick up on changes, especially if the changes are subtle, such as someone being quieter than normal or slowly going off their food. People are more likely to be referred to services if the changes in their behaviour cause problems to those around them, such as if they involve being aggressive or the destruction of property.

Often, there is a high staff turnover in services, and this can lead to staff having insufficient knowledge of the service user and not being able to recognise subtle changes in behaviour. Additionally, staff may have little experience or training on the mental health needs of people with learning disabilities. Without such experience, staff or carers may assume that such behaviour is due to the person having learning disabilities or may label it as challenging behaviour, without seeking its cause (see Chapter 7).

Compared to physical health problems, we know very little about the causes of mental health problems. The diagnosis of a physical condition is often straightforward, as blood tests, biopsies, x-rays and scans may make the diagnosis concrete. However, this is not the case for mental health problems – schizophrenia does not show up in a blood test and depression cannot be diagnosed by a brain scan.

Support staff and carers have to play have an important role to play in ensuring that people with learning disabilities gain the appropriate services for their mental health problems. It is crucial that support staff and carers are able to recognise changes in behaviour and act accordingly.

The prevalence of mental health problems in people with learning disabilities

Over the years, high rates of mental health problems have been reported in people with learning disabilities, ranging from 10% to 50%. The wide range reflects the variety of issues different researchers have regarded as mental health problems; some have included challenging behaviour and autistic spectrum disorders, and others have not.

Different populations have been studied (for example, those living in institutions or community samples). Recent studies have suggested that prevalence rates of mental health problems in people with learning disabilities are higher than in the general population, but not to the extent that was previously thought.

The principles of assessment

The assessment of mental health problems views the individual in a holistic way, taking into consideration not only the biological aspects but also the psychological and social aspects of the individual and their life, and how this has led to them developing a mental health problem (see vulnerability factors in Chapter 1). This is called the bio/psycho/social approach. It is applied not only when assessing someone's mental health problems, but also when developing an intervention package.

We are alerted to the possibility that a service user may have a mental health problem by:

- changes in behaviour that others can observe; these are called *signs* (examples: you can see if someone is more active than usual, if they are eating more or hurting themselves)

or

- changes internal to the person, distress or other sensations that are reported by the person and that only they can explain; these are called *symptoms* (examples: someone having feelings of paranoia or experiencing auditory hallucinations).

People with mild learning disabilities generally tend to display similar signs and symptoms to the general population. Assessment will also be similar, but there may be a greater reliance on information from others. People with more severe learning disabilities are more likely to show atypical signs and symptoms; changes are more likely to be behavioural in nature. Due to communication issues, it is very difficult to elicit information on internal changes such as psychotic experiences, and assessment will usually be based on observations.

Some physical health problems can produce a similar clinical presentation to mental health problems. People with learning disabilities are at a higher risk of poor physical health but they tend to use their GPs less than the rest of the population. Thus, any mental health assessment should rule out the possibility of a physical complaint. Special attention to the detection of sensory problems (such as hearing and sight) is essential, as these may contribute to the difficulties a person experiences.

Some people with learning disabilities engage in behaviour that is considered challenging. This may occur due to difficulties in communicating, environmental influences and the responses service users receive from those around them. But in some cases, it might indicate the presence of a mental health problem, especially when it is a new behaviour or an increase in frequency of existing behaviours. A mental health assessment should be sought.

Making a diagnosis

The basic clinical approach to making a diagnosis is to match the changes in the person to patterns of signs and symptoms that have been found to exist together in large groups of people with mental health problems. For example, someone who is experiencing the following is likely to be depressed:

- low or irritable mood

- lack of interest

- decreased energy

- loss of confidence or self-esteem

- sleep disturbance.

In schizophrenia, the classic signs and symptoms include delusions, hallucinations, difficulty arranging thoughts and the feeling of being taken over by an alien force. But schizophrenia is a very diverse mental health problem that can appear completely different from one person to another. Taking this into consideration, it is not surprising that clinicians do not always agree about the diagnosis of specific cases.

In order to align diagnostic criteria, systems have been developed to classify mental health problems (for example *International Classification of Diseases (ICD-10) and Diagnostic and Statistical Manual of Mental Disorders (DSM)*). These are based on psychopathology in the general population and do not take into consideration the altered trajectory of development or the presence of atypical symptomology (Hardy & Bouras, 2002). The Royal College of Psychiatrists (2001) recognised these problems and have produced the *DC-LD: Diagnostic Criteria for Psychiatric Disorders for Use with Adults with Learning Disabilities* to be used along side ICD–10.

Debate and discussion have always surrounded the use of 'psychiatric' diagnoses. There are both positive and negative aspects to receiving a diagnosis of a mental health problem, as shown in **Table 2.1**.

Table 2.1: Positive and negative aspects to receiving a diagnosis of a mental health problem	
Positive	**Negative**
• Correct diagnosis will lead to the correct treatment • Some service users need or like to have a diagnosis, something that explains the way they are feeling • May enable service users to relate with people who have similar experiences • Enables effective research • Enables government, commissioners and managers to plan services to meet users' needs	• Can alter other people's perceptions of the service user • Labels tend to stick • The service user can be defined by their diagnostic label • Can cause stigma and prejudice • May limit the person's opportunities

A diagnosis is only useful if it means positive action will be taken to help and support the service user. The person should not be defined by their diagnosis, as they are first and foremost a person. It should always be remembered that people can and do get better. Stigma should be addressed. It is society's perception of mental health problems that causes the negative response to a psychiatric diagnosis, and not the diagnosis itself.

Assessment

A diagnosis is made after a comprehensive mental health assessment has been completed. The process of assessment should be multidisciplinary, and will aim at answering the following questions:

• What is the problem?

• Why is it happening now?

• Has anything caused or contributed to the problem?

• Apart from managing the mental health problem, are there vulnerability factors that can be reduced to make relapse less likely? (See Chapter 1.)

• What does the service user want to do about the problem?

To answer these questions, a large amount of information about the person's current situation and their history needs to be gathered.

Table 2.2: Information required for a mental health assessment	
Current situation	**Historical information**
• What do the service user and staff/carer think the problem is? • Why are they seeking help now? • What is the person normally like? • What has changed? • Possible signs and symptoms of a mental health problem? • Recent life events or changes?	• Family • Personal • Medical • Psychiatric • Personality

Information about the current situation will be elicited by interviewing the person with learning disabilities and, if appropriate, staff/carers. The clinician should seek the service user's consent to approach staff/carers. Rules of good interviewing of people with learning disabilities are not fundamentally different from those applicable to the general population. There are, however, some particular points the clinician will need to consider. People with learning disabilities are more likely to say whatever they believe the interviewer wants to hear, especially if they perceive the other person to be in a position of authority. The clinician may need to ask the same question in a different way at a later stage, to check they correctly understand the situation. Some people may have a relatively short span of attention, so several short interviews may have to occur over a period of time and in whatever environment the person feels most comfortable. It is preferable that open-ended questions are used, as people may be easily suggestible, especially when leading questions are used, or they may feel under pressure. When eliciting the symptoms of mental illness, the clinician needs to gauge when the problem started and for how long it has been occurring. People with learning disabilities may have difficulties with the concept of time and dates. A useful tool is to use anchor events in the person's life, such as birthdays, Christmas or regular activities. Interviewers should consider how the person communicates and their level of understanding. For example, people with autism may have great difficulty in understanding abstract concepts such as emotion-related words. So asking someone 'How do you feel today?' might not be appropriate. Different tools can be used to enhance understanding, such as symbols, pictures, and photographs.

The history is often the key to finding out what the problem (ie the diagnosis) is; for example, knowing that someone is having difficulty sleeping, has lost weight, is irritable and is refusing to join in their normal activities, may point the to a diagnosis of depression. The history also helps the clinician understand the possible causes of the problem and how the individual came to this point in their life. For example, the person may have been abused as a teenager, had a series of losses in early adulthood and has always had trouble in developing friendships. This information influences the intervention plan. For example, counselling may be recommended for the abuse and losses; and the relapse prevention strategy may include social skills training to help the person develop friendships.

Assessment tools

Over recent years, a number of tools have been developed to assist in the detection of mental health problems in people with learning disabilities. One of the most widely used screening tools is the Psychiatric Assessment Schedule for Adults with Developmental Disabilities Checklist (PAS-ADD) (Moss, 2002). The PAS-ADD checklist can be used by support staff and carers. The staff member or carer is asked to rate if the person has shown any of 29 identifiable psychiatric symptoms in the previous four weeks. If the person scores over a certain threshold, then it is recommended that they seek a mental health assessment. It is quick and easy to administer and is written in non-technical language. It should be noted that the checklist is not a diagnostic tool.

Conclusion

The assessment of mental health problems in people with learning disabilities can often pose difficulties for those involved. But with a co-ordinated, multidisciplinary approach that takes into consideration the psychological and social dimensions, as well as the biological dimensions, a comprehensive holistic assessment can be achieved.

References and further reading

American Psychiatric Association (1994) *Diagnostic and Statistical Manual IV.* Arlington: American Psychiatric Publishing Inc.

Cooper SA (2003) Classification and Assessment of Psychiatric Disorders in Adults with Learning Disabilities. *Psychiatry* **2** (8) 12–16.

Deb S, Matthews T, Holt G & Bouras N (2001) *Practice Guidelines for the Assessment and Diagnosis of Mental Health Problems in Adults with Intellectual Disability.* Brighton: Pavilion Publishing.

Hardy S & Bouras N (2002) The presentation and assessment of mental health problems in people with learning disabilities. *Learning Disability Practice* **5** (3) 33–38.

Holt G, Gratsa A, Bouras N, Joyce T, Spiller MJ & Hardy S (2004) *Guide to Mental Health for Families and Carers of People with Intellectual Disabilities.* London: Jessica Kingsley.

Moss S (2002) *The Mini PAS-ADD Interview Pack.* Brighton: Pavilion Publishing.

Priest H & Gibbs M (2004) *Mental Health Care for People with Learning Disabilities.* Oxford: Churchill Livingstone.

Royal College of Psychiatrists (2001) *DC-LD: Diagnostic Criteria for Psychiatric Disorders for Use with Adults with Learning Disabilities/Mental Retardation.* London: Gaskell.

World Health Organisation (1993) *The ICD-10 Classification of Mental and Behavioural Disorders: Clinical Descriptions and Diagnostic Guidelines.* Geneva: World Health Organisation.

CHAPTER THREE

Biological interventions

ROB WINTERHALDER AND CAROL PATON

Introduction

This chapter is concerned with the use of medications commonly prescribed for people with learning disabilities and psychiatric or behavioural disorders; their indications for use, the side effects to look out for and how to overcome these. The information given in this chapter is geared to help support workers to understand the basics about medication so that they can support service users better, and to help them to recognise when a problem may be medication-related, and when to contact the general practitioner (GP) or psychiatrist.

Classes

The medication most commonly prescribed in learning disabilities by psychiatrists fall into the following classes:

- antipsychotics (sometimes called neuroleptics or major tranquillisers), such as haloperidol and risperidone

- antidepressants, such as fluoxetine

- mood-stabilising medication, such as lithium

- anti-epileptics, which can sometimes be used as mood stabilisers, such as sodium valproate
- anxiolytic and hypnotic medication (sometimes called minor tranquillisers), such as diazepam and zopiclone.

Names

Service users and their carers usually know the proprietary name of a drug, such as Prozac or Risperdal. This is the name given by the company which manufactures the medication. These names are designed to be pronounced and remembered more easily. The name used by the doctor is the generic name. For example, the generic name for Prozac is 'fluoxetine' and the generic name for Risperdal is 'risperidone'. The generic name is written on the prescription and allows the pharmacist to supply the drug in the cheapest way to the NHS and substitute another brand if the first is not available for any reason.

In this chapter, the generic names of medication have been used.

Classes of medication

1. Antipsychotics

Examples

Older (sometimes called typical or traditional) antipsychotics:

- haloperidol (Serenace)
- chlorpromazine (Largactil)
- trifluoperazine (Stelazine)
- flupenthixol (Depixol injection).

Newer (usually called atypical) antipsychotics:
- olanzapine (Zyprexa)
- risperidone (Risperdal)
- quetiapine (Seroquel).

Uses

In general, the main use of these medications is in the treatment of psychoses; hence, they are grouped together and called antipsychotics. Antipsychotics are used in the treatment of disorders such as schizophrenia and mania (elevated mood). For a first episode of schizophrenia, the antipsychotic is usually prescribed for approximately a year after the individual has recovered, to reduce the risk of relapse. The majority of people who stop taking antipsychotics soon after recovery will become unwell again. Individuals who have relapsed may need to be on antipsychotics for longer.

Antipsychotics are also used in the emergency control of severe behaviour disturbances, to calm the service user and minimise the risk of harm to self or to others. These medications can sometimes be used in the short-term control of anxiety. Finally, these drugs are used to treat certain symptoms that may develop in people who are suffering with dementia (for example, agitation, hyperactivity, delusions, hallucinations and aggressive behaviour). Antipsychotics are not addictive – that is, people do not develop a craving for them.

Side effects

Antipsychotics may have some unwanted side effects, which must be weighed against their benefits. Not all service users will develop all the possible side effects associated with a particular drug. Indeed, some may develop none. The following side effects may be associated with antipsychotics as a group.

Sometimes, soon after starting the medication, service users may develop stiffness, develop a tremor of their fingers and dribble saliva. These symptoms are similar to those experienced by people who have Parkinson's disease and are therefore called Parkinsonian symptoms. Anticholinergic medication (sometimes called anti-Parkinsonian or anti-muscarinic) such as procyclidine (Kemadrin) or orphenadrine (Disipal) are then given to treat these side effects. Anticholinergic medications have their own side effects, such as dry mouth, constipation, urine retention and blurred vision. The side effects of antipsychotics may decline with time or if the dose of antipsychotic is reduced. To complicate matters further, antipsychotics themselves may cause anticholinergic side effects (in which case they may be less likely to cause Parkinsonian side effects!).

Another side effect of antipsychotics, which may be noticeable soon after starting the medication, is that the service user becomes restless and fidgety. This restlessness especially affects the legs and has been described as an inability to sit still. It is known as akathisia.

Abnormal face and body movements may occur *soon* after starting antipsychotics. Service users may clench the jaw, protrude their tongue or, rarely, have an acute dystonic reaction whereby their head and body are rigidly bent backwards, the eyes are rolled upwards and the tongue is sticking out of their mouth. The treatment for acute dystonia is to give an anticholinergic drug immediately. If the service user has difficulty swallowing, he or she may need an intramuscular injection of a drug like procyclidine. In that case, take the service user to casualty.

Some antipsychotics are less likely to cause these side effects. Newer antipsychotics such as olanzapine (Zyprexa) and quetiapine (Seroquel) are much better in this respect than older medication such as haloperidol. It is therefore important to review medication and try to change to a different antipsychotic medication to reduce or stop these side effects.

Service users who have been taking antipsychotics for *many years* (usually at least five years) may develop tardive dyskinesia – abnormal face and body movements characterised by chewing and sucking movements, grimacing and slow, turning movements of the head and limbs. These are a social handicap that may improve after stopping the medication. The only treatment is prevention. Antipsychotics should be taken at as low a dose and for as short a time as possible.

Most antipsychotic drugs can also cause the amount of prolactin (a hormone) to rise in the body. Effects of this are most noticeable in women, as periods can stop and breast milk can be produced. If you think this may be happening to a service user, tell the doctor. Raised prolactin may also cause sexual problems.

Some of these medications can lower blood pressure (especially chlorpromazine, but olanzapine rarely causes this problem). Service users will complain of feeling dizzy when they get up from their bed or chair, and may fall and hurt themselves. The elderly are particularly susceptible. Fortunately, the dizziness usually disappears after the service user has been on the medication for a few weeks. Some of these medications may also cause abnormal heart rhythms leading to palpitations, faints etc.

Service users who are treated with these medications tend to put on excessive amounts of weight, because the medication increases appetite. It may be wise to help service users to control their weight. Weight gain can lead to diabetes. If a service user seems to be very thirsty, is passing water often, is more tired than normal or seems to be confused, tell the doctor.

Many people with learning disabilities suffer with epilepsy. Antipsychotic medication tends to worsen epilepsy and the anti-epileptic medication may have to be increased to compensate for this.

All antipsychotics can also cause side effects that are peculiar to that medication. For example, chlorpromazine can cause skin photosensitivity and pigmentation, which means that the service user is more likely to burn in the sun. Thus, service users taking chlorpromazine must apply sunscreen before going out in the sun. Olanzapine can cause swollen legs (this is rare) and risperidone can cause a runny nose.

Depot injections

In addition to the usual route of taking medication orally, some of these medications may be given by injection into the buttock every two, three or four weeks (none of the other classes of psychotropic medication, eg antidepressants, come in a depot form). They are formulated to be absorbed slowly from this site. This method is good for those who are not reliable with taking oral medication. However, this is not the method to use if the dose needs to be altered frequently.

Examples of depot medication are flupenthixol (Depixol), zuclopenthixol (Clopixol) and haloperidol (Haldol). Risperidone (Risperdal Consta) is the only atypical antipsychotic currently available in a depot form. This medication must be given every two weeks. The frequency of administration of the other depots is more flexible.

2. Antidepressants

Examples

- Tricyclic antidepressants: amitriptyline (Tryptizol), dothiepin (Prothiaden)
- Selective serotonin reuptake inhibitor antidepressants: sertraline (Lustral), fluoxetine (Prozac)
- Monoamine oxidase inhibitors (MAOIs): phenelzine (Nardil)
- Newer antidepressants: venlafaxine (Efexor), mirtazepine (Zispin), reboxetine (Edronax)

Uses

Antidepressants are indicated for the treatment of major depressive disorders. They start to lift mood after approximately a couple of weeks. Once the person is well, the tablets should be taken for at least six months before they are gradually withdrawn.

They can also be used for service users who are severely debilitated by generalised anxiety, phobias and panic attacks.

Some SSRI antidepressants are also licensed for use in obsessive compulsive disorder and bulimia nervosa.

Side effects

(a) Tricyclic (TCA) antidepressants

These older antidepressants tend to be sedative. This is beneficial in many cases of depression, where the service user is anxious and agitated in addition to being depressed. The antidepressant then calms the service user and helps him or her to sleep. In fact, this calming effect becomes evident almost at once, whereas the antidepressant effect takes about two weeks to start.

Common complaints include dry mouth, constipation, blurred vision and sweating. These medications also stimulate the appetite, which may be an advantage in those who have lost weight due to their depression. Like the antipsychotics, they lower blood pressure and cause dizziness, especially when posture is altered.

People who may be already unsteady on their feet, like the elderly and disabled, are particularly susceptible to falls due to this dizziness. These antidepressants may also worsen heart problems and cause palpitations. In addition, they lower the epilepsy threshold and the number of fits may increase.

(b) Selective serotonin reuptake inhibitor (SSRI) antidepressants

The efficacy of the SSRIs is similar to the TCAs. The advantage of these newer antidepressants is that they are less likely to cause dry mouth, blurred vision and constipation, and to affect the heart and blood pressure. They are also safer in overdose. Instead of being sedative, they may cause restlessness. Some cause nausea and vomiting and may reduce appetite, causing weight loss. With both the TCAs and SSRIs, most of the side effects become less noticeable after a while.

(c) Monoamine oxidase inhibitors (MAOIs)

MAOIs are rarely used because they can cause dangerous symptoms including a rise in blood pressure (if severe – an early warning sign might be a headache) when taken with certain foods, such as cheese or Bovril, and medication, such as cough mixtures. Phenelzine (Nardil) is used more often than tranylcypromine. If a service user is taking MAOIs make sure that you get an information leaflet from the pharmacy.

More recently, a reversible MAOI, moclobemide, has been developed, which is safer in this respect with less restrictions on diet.

(d) Newer antidepressants

Several new antidepressants have become available in the last few years. They are all equally effective but have different side effects. Venlafaxine can cause nausea and can raise blood pressure when it is given in higher doses. Mirtazepine can cause sedation and weight gain. Reboxetine can cause insomnia.

3. Mood-stabilising medications

Examples

- Lithium (Priadel, Camcolit, etc.)
- Carbamazepine (Tegretol)
- Sodium valproate (Epilim)

Lithium

Uses

People who suffer with manic–depressive psychosis may need a mood stabiliser to stabilise their mood. These people get depressed and need antidepressants to lift their mood, but their mood may suddenly swing the other way to became manic, needing antipsychotics. To prevent these swings in mood, which are so disruptive, service users are prescribed a mood stabiliser. Mood stabilisers may reduce the number of episodes of low or high mood, decrease the severity of the episodes or make the episodes shorter. Sometimes a depressive illness is resistant to other forms of treatment, and lithium may be added to antidepressants to lift this depression. It is also used to lower the mood of those with hypomania.

Monitoring

Lithium is taken on a long-term basis to prevent relapses. It is an effective medication but has potentially serious side effects. Before starting on the medication, service users need to have blood tests to make sure that their kidneys and thyroid are working properly. Once the blood level of the drug has been stabilised (0.5–1 mmol/l), blood tests are then done at about six-monthly intervals to check that the dose of lithium is right for the service user and that their kidneys and thyroid are still working properly. If the level of lithium in the blood is too high, kidney damage may occur. In practice, because of the close monitoring of service users on lithium, serious side effects are very rare.

Apart from lithium and some anticonvulsants, it is not routine practice to check blood levels of drugs. Because of the need to closely monitor lithium with blood tests, service users with learning disabilities who are not compliant with blood tests, are not usually prescribed lithium. If a mood stabiliser is required, drugs such as carbamazepine and sodium valproate may be considered.

Side effects

Side effects which are immediately noticeable include nausea, loose bowels, tiredness, fine tremor, feeling thirsty and passing a lot of urine. These may improve after a while.

Chronic side effects include tremor, weight gain, slight forgetfulness and excessive drinking and passing a lot of urine. Some people on lithium become hypothyroid (that is, their thyroid gland is underactive) and need to be treated with thyroxine.

Toxicity

Toxicity occurs when the blood level of lithium is too high (above 1.5 mmol/l). This may occur if the service user becomes dehydrated – due to diarrhoea and vomiting, for example – or if he or she is unable to drink a normal amount.

When toxicity occurs, the service user may experience the following: appetite loss, vomiting, diarrhoea, coarse tremor, slurred speech, unsteadiness on his or her feet, sleepiness and seizures. Eventually coma and death may occur.

Carbamazepine

Carbamazepine is generally used for the treatment of epilepsy, but more recently, it has been used to stabilise mood disorders. Although lithium is thought to be more effective, carbamazepine has the advantage of having fewer side effects. Sometimes, if lithium is not effective at controlling mood fluctuations, then carbamazepine is added. Carbamazepine is also sometimes used to control challenging behaviour. Both carbamazepine and sodium valproate (below) are discussed in greater detail in Chapter 8: Epilepsy.

Sodium valproate (Epilim)

Sodium valproate is used to treat many different types of epilepsy and is also an effective mood stabilising medication. It is more effective in treating and preventing mania (high mood) than depression (low mood).

4. Hypnotics and anxiolytics

(a) Benzodiazepines

Examples

- Diazepam (Valium)
- Nitrazepam (Mogadon)
- Lorazepam (Ativan)
- Temazepam

Uses

Benzodiazepines have both hypnotic (induce sleep) and anxiolytic (reduce anxiety) properties. They are useful for a few days, but the cause of the insomnia or anxiety must be tackled. Service users may become addicted to them, experiencing unpleasant withdrawal symptoms when they are stopped.

Lorazepam can also be used for the control of acutely disturbed behaviour, as it is rapidly sedative when given by injection. Other benzodiazepines can be given orally if the service user will accept them.

Some benzodiazepines like clonazepam (Rivotril) and diazepam (Stesolid) are used to control epilepsy. They can also help in the withdrawal from other drugs, such as alcohol.

Side effects

These medications differ in the length of time they are active. For example, temazepam is active for about eight hours and is therefore useful to help people sleep, whereas diazepam stays in the blood for much longer and is used to reduce anxiety. A common side effect is drowsiness, which leads to poor concentration and decreases the service user's ability to learn. This side effect may be dangerous if the service user has to be able to react quickly, for example, when crossing the road.

After a few weeks, the service user may develop a tolerance for the medication (ie the same dose no longer has the desired effect and more has to be taken to get the same effect). The service user very quickly becomes addicted to the medication and, although the same dose no longer relieves anxiety, stopping the medication can make the service user feel even more anxious, restless, unable to sleep, sweaty, confused, prone to headaches and craving for the medication. Weaning an addicted person from hypnotics can be a slow, difficult process.

Taking too much benzodiazepine may cause intoxication; the service user may become unsteady and drowsy, and may slur their speech.

(b) Non-benzodiazepines

Examples

- Zopiclone (Zimovane)
- Buspirone (Buspar)

Zopiclone is used for the short–term treatment of insomnia. Buspirone is used for the short–term treatment of anxiety.

Side effects

Side effects of zopiclone may include a bitter or metallic taste, nausea and vomiting, dry mouth and irritability. Side effects of buspirone may include nausea, dizziness, headache and nervousness.

Choice of medication

Which medication is prescribed depends on the disorder being treated, any prominent symptoms and compliance issues. The medications differ in the range of disorders in which they are effective, their sedative properties, and side effects.

How medications work

Inside the brain there are hundreds of millions of nerve fibres. These nerve fibres communicate with each other, not by touching, but by sending chemical messengers from one nerve fibre to the next. Different chemical messengers have different jobs. For example, if too much dopamine (a chemical messenger) is sent from one nerve fibre to the next, psychotic symptoms such as hallucinations may occur. If there is too little serotonin (another chemical messenger), depression may result. There are dozens of chemical messengers in the brain and each group of medication targets a different one or different combination.

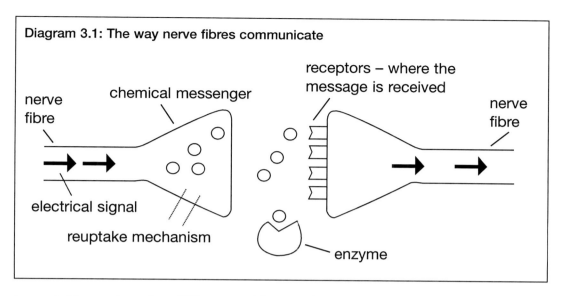

Diagram 3.1: The way nerve fibres communicate

In each illness, there is a different problem with under- or over-activity of these communication channels. The aim of medication is to correct this underlying problem. For example, antipsychotic drugs work by reducing the activity of dopamine, and antidepressants work by increasing the activity of serotonin or noradrenaline, or both. Unfortunately, these actions by medication on chemical messengers are also responsible for some side effects.

Because no two medications have exactly the same effect on nerve fibres, people may respond well to one medication but not to another that is very similar. Choosing the right medication from a group is often a matter of trial and error, as it cannot be predicted who will respond.

Use of medication in challenging behaviour

When psychosocial interventions in a case of severe challenging behaviour have failed, it may be necessary to intervene with psychotropic medication. There are three ways in which psychotropic medication may help:

1. In a non-specific manner, by reducing the service user's agitation and calming them.

2. In a specific way, targeting abnormally functioning chemical messenger systems in the brain which are thought to contribute to the challenging behaviour.

3. Medication may also work by treating an underlying mental illness which has not been recognised as contributing to the challenging behaviour.

Some behaviours, such as over-activity, aggression and ritualistic behaviour (which are sometimes seen in people with learning disabilities, and particularly those who also have autism) may respond to antipsychotic medication. Antipsychotics may also calm agitated service users and treat aggression and stereotypies; antidepressants have been used to treat self-injurious behaviour, ritualistic behaviours etc, and mood stabilisers may be indicated for aggression or self-injurious behaviour. It is less clear how long psychotropic medication should be prescribed for, in a case of challenging behaviour not due to mental illness. Regardless, it is good practice periodically to review the need for ongoing psychotropic medication.

National standards for administration of medication in care homes

Whether a care home is large or small, and whether or not the staff have a nursing qualification, there is a duty of care placed on the employer and the carers that requires medication to be safely handled so that the people who are cared for are supported to take their medication safely. For a care home member of staff to administer a medication, the medication must have a printed label containing the following information:

- service user's name
- date of dispensing
- name and strength of medication
- dose and frequency of medication.

A service user information leaflet must be supplied with each medication (including those supplied in monitored dosage systems), and these should be made available to the service user (where appropriate).

The use of complimentary/alternative treatments, as with other treatments, should only be undertaken with the expressed agreement of the service user, or person who is authorised to speak on the service user's behalf. Advice should always be sought from the pharmacist about any potential interactions between the non-prescription medication and the service user's regular medication.

It is the responsibility of the registered manager to ensure that staff access training that meets basic requirements. Where care home staff are required to administer medication by an invasive route (for example, administration of rectal Diazepam), additional training will be necessary. This training should incorporate an assessment of competence on a service user specific basis.

Mental Health in Learning Disabilities **A reader** © Pavilion Publishing (Brighton) Ltd 2005

Service users should be supported and facilitated to take control of and manage their own health care, including support to manage their own medical conditions where feasible. The registered manager and staff should encourage and support service users to retain, administer and control their own medication, within a risk management framework, and comply with the home's policy and procedure for the receipt, recording, storage, handling, administration and disposal of medication.

In residential care homes, all medication, including controlled drugs (except those for self-administration) should be administered by designated and appropriately trained staff. The training for care staff must be accredited and include:

- basic knowledge of how medications are used and how to recognise and deal with problems in use
- the principles behind all aspects of the home's policy on handling medication and records.

The role of carers is summarised in **Box 3.1**.

Box 3.1: The role of carers

- Make sure you know:
  - what the medication is expected to do
  - what the side effects might be
  - how long it needs to be taken for.

- Ensure the service user takes the medication as prescribed.

- Tell the doctor if the service user seems to be having side effects.

- Keep a list of all the medication the service user is receiving.

- Take it with you each time the service user sees a doctor (GP, psychiatrist etc), or if you buy any medication from a pharmacy.

- If you have any questions at all about any of the medication the service user is taking, ask the doctor or pharmacist.

Conclusion

It is important to remember that medication should be used as part of a management programme. For instance, a person who has a depressive illness may have their mood lifted with an antidepressant but, for the person to make a full recovery, any stresses which precipitated the depression should be resolved.

Attention to psychological and environmental factors may also help prevent a relapse.

The medications discussed in this chapter are a selection of common medications used by psychiatrists, but it has by no means covered all of them. Nor are all the examples of medication, given in order to illustrate points, the best medication of their class. Other doctors may prescribe another medication of that class because they are more familiar with its potency and side effects, or because that medication best meets the needs of a particular service user.

If a carer has concerns regarding medication, initially they should discuss this with their supervisor or line manager where relevant. If appropriate, these concerns should then be shared with the prescribing doctor or pharmacist.

References and further reading

Department of Health (2001) *Valuing People: A New Strategy for Learning Disabilities for 21st Century*. London: HMSO.

Department of Health (2000) *Care Homes for Adults (18–65). National Minimum Standards. Care Homes Regulations Second Edition. Care Standards Act*. London: HMSO.

Royal Pharmaceutical Society of Great Britain (2003) *The Administration and Control of Medicines in Care Homes and Children's Services*. London: Royal Pharmaceutical Society of Great Britain.

Information

The National Institute for Mental Health in England
Web: www.nimhe.org.uk

North Mersey Community NHS Trust, Well Informed
Web: www.northmersey.nhs.uk/informed/index.htm

National Care Standards Commission for England
Web: www.carestandards.gov.uk

CHAPTER **FOUR**

Psychological interventions for people with learning disabilities

BARLEY OLIVER AND PENNY SMITH

Aim

This chapter aims to help support staff to learn to identify when it is appropriate to refer an individual service user to a psychology service because of their emotional and psychological problems. The reasoning and theories underlying the different psychological intervention models will be briefly explained. The types of problems that might be helped by psychological interventions will be considered and the ways service users might benefit from different types of interventions will be discussed. Ways of introducing a service user to the idea of being referred to a psychology service and how to explain what this might entail will be explored. The implementation of the different stages of a psychological intervention with service users will be considered. Finally, an example of a psychological formulation will be given.

Introduction to psychological interventions

The provision of talking therapies for service users with learning disabilities has occurred only relatively recently, because in the past there has been an assumption that they would be unable to make use of them. This assumption was identified as 'therapeutic disdain' (Bender, 1993) and has gradually been replaced by the realisation that therapies offered to people without learning disabilities can also be helpful to people with learning disabilities, although each approach may need to be adapted for this service user group. There is a lack of research to determine the effectiveness of different types of interventions, possibly as a result of their limited use until the last decade (Hatton, 2002). There is also a significant lack of information about the suitability, level of preparedness or skill needed by service users to make sense of therapy and to benefit from it.

Psychological models of intervention

Currently, the psychological interventions most often used are; the behavioural approach, cognitive behavioural therapy, the systemic approach, non–directive counselling and psychodynamic therapy. Each of these therapy approaches will be considered, to determine the theory underlying each model and how this influences the therapy process.

The behavioural approach

The behavioural approach was the main psychological intervention available from psychology services for many years and as a result has been the most researched approach. This model is still the most likely intervention to be used with people with severe learning disabilities who significantly challenge services by the way they behave. This is because these service users tend to have little verbal communication and therefore cannot make use of talking therapies.

The behavioural approach is based on operant theory that assumes behaviour is learned as a result of positive or negative reinforcements (Murphy, 1994). Positive reinforcement is some kind of reward – an event the individual finds pleasurable. Negative reinforcement is when something the person finds unpleasant is removed or stops. With this model, service users' behaviour is understood by a functional analysis which considers the roles of the antecedents ('A') or setting events; a description of the behaviour ('B'), for example, its frequency; and the consequences ('C') of the behaviour. Over the last 40 years, the behavioural approach has developed from being mainly a behaviour modification approach where the goal was to remove or alter behaviours, to being a more sensitive and constructive approach. An attempt is made to understand the behaviour from the service user's perspective, to find out what is maintaining it and to help the individual develop more adaptive strategies to achieve the same goal. Only observable behaviour is objectively analysed. The individual's thoughts, ideas and feelings are not taken into account, as they cannot be directly accessed.

Cognitive behavioural therapy

In the last decade, this approach has been offered more frequently to service users with learning disabilities. However, for it to be successful, it is suggested that individuals need to be able to make sense of certain causal relationships such as the consequences of an event. The suggestion that a certain level of preparedness is necessary makes common sense, but there is still a scarcity of research to inform therapists about how to assess if someone is able enough to engage in this type of therapy.

Cognitive behavioural therapy (CBT) developed out of the behavioural approach, and emphasises the importance of an individual's cognitions – thoughts, ideas, beliefs, memories, perceptions and all the things that go on in people's minds. Inner processes are therefore considered to be of great importance. The main principle is that an individual is not disturbed by the event itself but by the meaning they attach to the event. CBT assumes that thoughts and beliefs influence emotions and behaviour. Emotional problems such as anxiety and depression arise from negative thoughts and beliefs and therefore can be helped by a change to more adaptive or positive thoughts and beliefs. CBT is based on learning theory so another important assumption it that an individual's beliefs and the way they view the world is learned, and therefore can be unlearned.

CBT uses strategies such as identifying and challenging negative thoughts, goal setting, relaxation and helping the individual to make positive statements about themselves.

The systemic model

In the last decade, the systemic approach has gradually begun to be introduced to services for people with learning disabilities. This approach considers the person as part of their social context. To change the person, there needs to be a change in their existing context (Minuchin, 1979). This model leads to the therapist posing hypotheses about the relationship between the service user and the social context, rather than to inner processes. What psychiatry would describe as 'signs' or 'symptoms' are in fact behaviours created to provide solutions to family or system problems. The therapy focuses on the individual and shared beliefs, behaviours and practices within the family, and how they affect the success of the family over time. The therapist's role is to facilitate a new pattern of interaction within the family relationships to resolve the presenting problem.

This approach can be used in family therapy and work with couples. It can also be used to bring about change in an organisation such as a staffed house. For service users with learning disabilities all these applications may be useful.

Non-directive counselling or person centred therapy

This approach is based on the assumption that a therapist can be of most help to service users by allowing them to find their own solutions to their problems. The emphasis with this approach is that the service user is the expert and the therapist acts as the source of reflection and encouragement. Person–centred counselling assumes that emotional problems are a result of a person's experience being denied, defined or discounted by others. People with learning disabilities are likely to have had such negative reactions to their experiences. Some of the important conditions to this type of therapy are that the therapist must give unconditional positive regard to the service user and offer empathic understanding to the service user.

This model can be a powerful approach for people with learning disabilities, whose voices are often ignored and whose experiences are often discounted.

Psychodynamic therapy

This approach evolved from the works of Freud, who believed that psychological disorders resulted from conflicts, usually in childhood, about which the person is unaware. There is an emphasis on the past and on the unconscious. The main aim is to bring the unconscious (repressed emotions and motives) into consciousness. The way the service user relates to the therapist is of great importance and the therapist is there to interpret material brought to each therapy session by the service user. Psychodynamic therapists talk of the primary and secondary handicaps associated with disability (eg Sinason, 1986). They describe the primary handicap as the actual physical, intellectual or emotional disability and the secondary handicap as the effect the primary handicap has on the person. There has been very little research about how helpful this form of therapy is for people with learning disabilities who, by definition, have problems understanding abstract concepts. The literature that does exist is often in the form of case studies but more recently, research has begun to be published that aims to be more rigorous (Beail, 1998).

Problems that may be helped by psychological interventions

A whole range of problems may be helped by a psychological intervention for this service user group: depression, substance misuse, eating disorders, anxiety, phobias, compulsions, loss and grief issues, relationship problems and psychotic symptoms such as hearing voices. Interventions are often provided alongside other types of interventions such as psychotropic medication, a change in environment (for example, to a different residential placement) or a change in levels of support. People with learning disabilities often have great difficulty in describing their mental state accurately, so diagnosing, classifying and successfully treating their mental health problems can be problematic (Hatton, 2002). Integrated multidisciplinary working with agreed goals and a co-ordinated approach is therefore crucial.

Issues that need to be addressed before therapy begins

For all assessments and psychological interventions, informed consent and confidentiality need to be carefully considered. With this service user group, both of these concepts are complex and often difficult to implement. For instance, it is not easy to determine if an individual has given *informed consent* and that, for example, they understand fully the implications of any treatment package and what may happen if they either accept it or refuse it. Someone who has a compulsive disorder and learning disabilities may not be able to understand the degree to which their lives are being restricted by the condition. Confidentiality is also problematic as there is a great need for the different agencies and professions to communicate and co-ordinate their work, but this can mean very sensitive and private information about an individual becomes known to a large group of people, including family members. This service user group is particularly susceptible to suggestibility and acquiescence, and have often not been given many opportunities to experience choice. For these reasons, there is a need to think about these issues with each individual and weigh up the extent to which they are able to give informed consent about interventions and with whom information should be shared (see Chapter 10).

How clinical interventions are implemented

Generally, for all the psychological approaches discussed in this chapter (with the possible exception of the psychodynamic model), the psychologist will follow three stages during the implementation of an intervention. The first stage will be the assessment period, when information is gathered from several sources. If possible, information will be gathered from the service user in terms of how they see the problem, how this affects their life and what thoughts or beliefs they have in relation to the problem. Carers, both paid and unpaid, will be asked how they see the problem, and what they believe are the causes. Sometimes the psychologist will directly observe the service user in a structured way to add more information to the assessment.

The second stage is when a clinical formulation is developed on the basis of all the information that has been collected. This will clarify what the setting events are that have led to the problem developing, what the maintaining factors are that mean that the problem continues and how this is manifested in the individual's thoughts and behaviours. The formulation informs the intervention plan and how it will be implemented.

It is important to evaluate any clinical interventions, and this is usually done in a variety of ways. The frequency of a problematic behaviour might be measured over time to see if it changes, and this may be measured through direct observations or by the service user or support staff recording when it happens. The service user might be asked to report on a regular basis how they believe they are progressing, possibly using a self-report questionnaire or with the use of simplified mood charts or diaries.

An example of a formulation

Maria is a 25–year-old woman who lives with her parents. She chooses not to attend any daytime or evening activities. She has no friends. If she is asked, she says she does not want to go to any social events. She is tearful, quiet and appears anxious if she is taken to a social event, and she is sometimes sick which results in her having to go home earlier than planned.

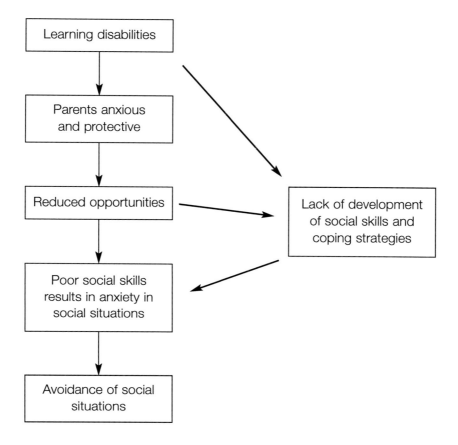

A formulation can be used by the psychologist to help the service user and their carer(s) think about the situation in a comprehensive way and to consider how different factors are affecting the clinical problem. The intervention plan is developed on the basis of the formulation. For example, the formulation above suggests that an intervention plan might focus on Maria's needs in a number of ways. The social situations Maria finds difficult could be explored and then she could be helped through techniques like relaxation and role play to develop better coping strategies and social skills. She could then be supported to gradually attend social events, starting with things she found the least difficult. Her parents might need support to develop confidence in letting her take part in activities without them.

Conclusion

Individual and group psychological therapies are widely used in mainstream mental health services for people without learning disabilities. There is now growing evidence that they are also very useful and effective for people with learning disabilities, and they should always be considered as part of a multidisciplinary intervention package.

References and further reading

Beail N (1998) Psychoanalytical psychotherapy with men with intellectual disabilities: A preliminary outcome study. *British Journal of Medical Psychology* 71, 1–11.

Bender M (1993) The unoffered chair: The history of therapeutic disdain towards people with learning disability. *Clinical Psychology Forum* 54, 7–12.

Hatton C (2002) Psychosocial interventions for adults with intellectual disabilities and mental health problems: A review. *Journal of Mental Health* **11** (4) 357–373.

Minuchin S (1979) *Families and Family Therapy*. London: Tavistock Publications.

Murphy G (1994) Understanding Challenging Behaviour. In: E Emerson, P McGill and J Mansell (Eds) *Severe Learning Disabilities and Challenging Behaviours – Designing high quality services*. London: Chapman and Hall.

Sinason V (1986) Secondary Mental Handicap and its Relationship to Trauma. *Psychoanalysis Psychotherapy* **2** (2) 131–154.

Stenford Kroese B, Dagnan D & Loumidis K (1997) *Cognitive Behaviour Therapy for People with Learning Disabilities*. London: Routledge.

CHAPTER FIVE

Social interventions

STEVE HARDY, PETER WOODWARD AND JANE BARNES
WITH CONTRIBUTIONS FROM THE TUESDAY GROUP, LEWISHAM

Introduction

The social needs of a person can be divided into four domains; the *individual* themselves, the place they call *home*, the *community* in which they live and how they spend their *day*. These four domains play a large role in the predisposing, precipitation and perpetuation of mental health problems in individuals. For example, in the general population there is good evidence to suggest that poor social support, measured as a lack of intimacy or social integration, is associated with an increased risk of depression (Paykel & Cooper, 1992). Gregory *et al* (2003) describe how social isolation and exclusion play a large part both in triggering and exacerbating mental ill health in people with learning disabilities. Thus, any intervention package for improving mental health should be holistic in nature. It should address not only the individual's biological and psychological needs but also their social needs.

No single profession or team alone can meet all the social needs of people with learning disabilities. A broad-based, multi-agency approach is required to deliver social interventions (Gregory *et al*, 2003), ensuring that a person–centred approach is adopted and that any intervention is developed in partnership with the individual. Along with biological and psychological interventions, the person's consent is also required for social interventions. Some professionals, such as social workers or care managers, will have specific responsibilities for social interventions, and other professionals may have the skills and experience to address particular needs.

1. Community Interventions

Supporting the person into an inclusive community

People with learning disabilities were for many years segregated from the rest of society, whether by living in institutions or by using separate services. Mental health care plans, along with any approach to people with learning disabilities, should promote inclusion. Inclusion means enabling people with learning disabilities to do ordinary things, make use of mainstream services and be fully included in the local community (Department of Health, 2001). Having a sense of connectedness with one's community is positive for an individual's mental health; it builds self-worth and self-esteem, and gives a feeling of belonging. Supporters of people with learning disabilities are responsible for promoting social inclusion. This involves supporting people to live in local communities, to use local amenities such as shops, leisure centres and colleges, to join groups and go to classes, and to join in local community campaigns.

> *'For most of us, community connections and involvement develop naturally during the course of daily life. This does not necessarily happen for people with learning difficulties. So it is important to deliberately plan a course of action that aims to achieve that goal.'*
>
> Cole and Lloyd, 2000

Having control over one's life and shaping one's own destiny helps improve mental health. Inclusion should also address service-related issues. People with learning disabilities and mental health problems should be informed and consulted about decision-making, and should participate in it, whether it be about their own care or about service development. People should be supported to use their voices, services should listen to what they say and change should occur because of what has been said.

Supporting the person to build their social networks

In 2003, the Tuesday Group (a mental health promotion group for people with learning disabilities) wrote a report called *Our Mental Health* (Tuesday Group, 2003). The report concluded that having a social life is important for mental health and that support staff should help people with learning disabilities increase their social networks. As people are included in community life, opportunities for widening social networks will hopefully increase. But for those with additional mental health needs, explicit plans may need to be made. These might include improving the individual's social skills, strategies to reduce social anxiety and accessing befriender schemes.

A major risk factor for depression is the lack of a close relationship and having no-one to confide in. The Tuesday Group also reported that having a relationship with someone special to share one's life with was important. This has often been a recognised but ignored need of people with learning disabilities. This has arisen not from neglect but from a wish to protect people who are potentially vulnerable. Services need to address this issue, sensitively supporting people to develop close relationships whilst ensuring they are not put at unacceptable risk.

2. Interventions based around the individual

People with learning disabilities are likely to have less developed life skills, such as socialising, coping and problem solving. These are necessary for the individual to recover, prevent relapse and reintegrate in society.

People with learning disabilities can be supported to develop skills. This can include:

- **Coping skills** – supporting the individual to recognise situations that may cause distress, and having a range of strategies to deal with them. A psychologist or occupational therapist would be most likely to provide this kind of support, with assistance from support staff and carers.

- **Social skills and communication** – develop the skills needed to socialise with other people and understand the complex rules of social interaction. These can include turn taking, recognising other people's emotions and applying social rules to different situations (ie the difference between work and the pub). A range of professionals, including speech and language therapists and psychologists, provide these interventions with support from carers and support staff.

- **Budgeting** – poverty is often associated with mental health problems and can be a contributing factor, consequence or both. Although the social worker or care manager will support the individual in receiving the appropriate benefits, the money received will have to be managed. Occupational therapists, with the support of carers and staff, can help the person develop budgeting skills.

- **Assertiveness** – low self-esteem and self-worth are often associated with poor mental health, and may result from the individual feeling unable to assert themselves. Psychologists and occupational therapists can support people to develop assertiveness skills.

The facilitation of life skill development may take place on an individual basis or in a group setting.

Providing opportunities at transitions and life's turning points

At one time or another, we are all faced with transitions. Some of these, such as finding a new job, we choose ourselves; others, such as leaving school or retiring, are imposed on us. Transitions can contribute to or be a consequence of poor mental health. Those with mental health problems may need to go into hospital or move home because their environment does not meet their needs.

Transitions that are of particular importance to people with learning disabilities include the journey from adolescence to adult life, leaving the family home, the closure or reprovision of day services, moving between residential services, changes in employment or entering old age. These transitions can have a negative impact on their lives. Poorly managed transitions become stressful events. Sensitively managed transitions with forward planning can minimise the effect of adverse changes and can turn situations into positive events.

Take, for example, a middle-aged person with learning disabilities who lives at home with their ageing parent and has minimal access to services. When their parent inevitably passes away, the person will not only have to deal with the trauma of the death of their parent, but also the loss of their principle care giver and the probable move from the family home. In this case, sensitive advance planning will provide opportunities to discuss and plan what will happen, including the wishes of both the individual and their parent, future service options such as residential or outreach support, and appropriate funding.

Many local authorities are now developing transition teams for adolescents with learning disabilities, which plan the transition in collaboration with the individual. For adults with learning disabilities, their social worker/care manager, along with other professionals, can provide support and planning.

Supporting people to find a voice

People with learning disabilities may have little control over their own lives, although almost all, including the most severely disabled, are capable of making choices and expressing their views (Department of Health, 2001). Cole (2002) describes how, if someone with learning disabilities also has a mental health problem, there is a strong risk that they will have even less say about what happens to them. People with additional mental health needs require support to get their message across. Most areas within the UK have self-advocacy and citizen advocacy services that can help empower people with learning disabilities.

3. Home interventions

The Foundation for People with Learning Disabilities (2003) held an inquiry into the mental health needs of young people with learning disabilities. They found that, time and time again, a serious deterioration in a young person's mental health was triggered by a change in their environment (in this instance, an important part of the solution was to find a suitable home). Home should be a place where you can escape from the world around you, where you feel safe, where you are happy to be and, above all, where you chose to be.

The environment should be tailored to the individual's requirements. Evidence has shown that the following characteristics can promote good mental health, and interventions should aim to achieve them:

- the person has a choice about where they live and whom they live with
- the person feels secure and safe from harm
- reasonable expectations are made of the person
- life within the home is predictable and stable
- those who share the home have an accepting and non-judgemental attitude
- there is encouragement to succeed in whatever the person chooses to do
- praise is given for achievements
- the person has responsibility within the home.

Some research has suggested that certain environments where there is 'high expressed emotion' can increase the risk of relapse for those with psychotic conditions, notably schizophrenia (Brown *et al*, 1962; Vaughn & Leff, 1976). High expressed emotion occurs when the individual is residing in an environment where they experience critical comments, emotional hostility and emotional over-involvement. Interventions can be aimed at family members or fellow residents and supporters to be less critical and pressurising (Priest & Gibbs, 2004).

4. Interventions: how the person spends their day

Studies have shown a link between unemployment and mental health problems in the general population (Fryer, 1995). Felce & Perry (1995) found that low levels of daytime activity was not just associated with institutional care but also with modern community-based homes for people with learning disabilities, with some service users only receiving assistance to do activities for 2.5% of the time. It is not only the level of activity that needs to be examined but also the quality, its meaning to the individual and their choice in participating. Individuals need a structured timetable of meaningful daytime activity, which can include employment, using day services and activities within the home and in the community.

Employment

Employment not only provides an income but also offers opportunities to increase feelings of self worth and self-esteem. It can give people a sense of belonging, a sense of responsibility and a chance to achieve, all of which are known protective factors against poor mental health. Having a job also provides opportunities to increase social networks and develop relationships with people without learning disabilities. But it is estimated that less than 10% of people with learning disabilities are in employment (Department of Health, 2001). Holding down a paid job may not be realistic for all people with learning disabilities, but services should do their utmost where this is a possibility. Many areas now have employment agencies for people with learning disabilities, which provide support in finding a job in the local community and in developing interview skills, and give on-the-job assistance until the person feels confident. Some areas have also developed sheltered employment schemes such as horticulture centres and catering services. A social worker or care manager can help people access these services.

Meaningful activities at the day service

For some, employment may not be the best way to fill their day. In these instances, day services may be appropriate. Day services are currently under going a period of modernisation. Traditionally, they have primarily been a source of respite for carers and offer segregated activities within a day centre. The modernisation programme will involve giving people access to real activities, which will enable them to develop their skills and potential, and focus on inclusive and integrated activities within the community (Department of Health, 2001). Day services may support people to access adult education programmes within mainstream colleges, and to access leisure pursuits such as swimming, visiting the gym or going to the library. Social workers or care managers can support people to access day services.

Activities in the home and community

People with learning disabilities, especially the more severely disabled, may spend a large amount of time in supported housing. Support staff often find it difficult to engage people in activities. This can lead to boredom, challenging behaviour, apathy and depression.

Support staff need to make explicit plans on how to effectively engage service users – failing to plan is planning to fail. This will involve finding out the person's likes and dislikes, how they communicate, what they can do for themselves, what they need support to do and what resources are available.

Interventions such as active support (Jones *et al*, 1996) have been specifically developed to increase activity engagement. Active support is where varying levels of support are matched to an individual's needs in order for them to participate in a full and active life, and develop new skills, interests, relationships and opportunities, through systematic planning.

Conclusion

Social interventions play a vital and pivotal role in mental health care. As we have seen, unmet social needs can contribute to and be a consequence of poor mental health, placing the individual in a vicious cycle of social exclusion. Ensuring social needs are met should not only be viewed as part of an intervention in those that are mentally unwell. Social interventions should not be static, but part of an ongoing mental health promotion strategy.

References and further reading

Brown GW, Monck EM, Carstairs GM & Wing JK (1962) Influence of family life on the course of schizophrenic illness. *British Journal of Preventive and Social Medicine* 16, 55–68.

Cole A (2002) *Include Us Too: Developing and Improving Services to meet the mental health needs of people with learning disabilities.* London: Mental Health Foundation.

Cole A & Lloyd A (2000) Its not what you know, it's who! *Living Well* **1** (1).

Department of Health (2001) *Valuing People: A New Strategy for Learning Disability for the 21st Century.* London: HMSO.

Felce D & Perry J (1995) The extent of support for ordinary living provided in staffed housing: the relationship between staffing levels, resident dependency, staff:resident interactions and resident activity patterns. *Social Science and Medicine* 40, 799–810.

Foundation for People with Learning Disabilities (2003) *Count Us In: The report of the committee of inquiry into meeting the mental health needs of young people with learning disabilities.* London: Mental Health Foundation.

Fryer D (1995) Labour Market disadvantage, deprivation and mental health. *Psychologist* **8** (6) 265–72.

Gregory M, Newbigging K, Cole A & Pearsall A (2003) *Working Together: Developing and providing services for people with learning disabilities and mental health problems.* London: Mental Health Foundation.

Jones E, Perry J, Lowe K, Allen D, Toogood S & Felce D (1996) *Active support: a handbook for planning daily activities and support arrangements for people with learning disabilities.* Cardiff: Welsh Centre for Learning Disabilities Applied Research Unit.

Paykel & Cooper (1992) cited in Gelder M, Gath D, Mayou R & Cowen P (Eds) (1997) *Oxford Textbook of Psychiatry.* Third Edition. Oxford: Oxford University Press.

Priest H & Gibbs M (2004) *Mental Health Care for People with Learning Disabilities.* London: Churchill Livingstone.

Tuesday Group (2003) *Our Mental Health: The support people with learning disabilities want for their mental health.* London: Estia Centre.

Vaughn CE & Leff JP (1976) The influence of family and social factors, the course of psychiatric illness. *British Journal of Psychiatry* 129, 125–137.

CHAPTER SIX

Service factors

STEVE HARDY AND NICK BOURAS

Introduction

Over the last four decades, there have been great changes in the way services are delivered to people with learning disabilities. The principle theme of change has been 'inclusion'. The 1960s signalled the beginning of the closure of institutions and community resettlement programmes, and more recently the emphasis has been towards people accessing mainstream services.

Yet for those people with learning disabilities who have additional mental health problems, the pathway to inclusion has been more difficult. They were often the last people to be resettled into the community. Many were placed in specialist units miles away from family and friends, and faced the 'double jeopardy' of falling between learning disability services and mental health services, with their needs going unmet. This chapter will describe current government policy, examine different service models and explore the advantages and disadvantages of accessing mainstream mental health services.

Policy

Each country in the United Kingdom has its own policy for people with learning disabilities. These are:

- England – *Valuing People* (Department of Health, 2001)
- Northern Ireland – *Equal Lives* (Department of Health and Social Security, 2004)
- Scotland – *Same As You* (Scottish Executive, 2000)
- Wales – *Fulfilling the Promises* (Welsh Office, 2001).

These policies cover all aspects of a person's life and needs, from childhood to old age. They address the mental health needs of people with learning disabilities to varying degrees, but all promote an agenda of inclusion, supporting people with learning disabilities in mainstream mental health services whenever possible. One example of national policy on the mental health needs of people with learning disabilities is *Valuing People*, which states that:

- wherever possible, people are to use mainstream mental health services, both community and in-patient

- for those people who use mental health services, the Care Programme Approach (CPA) should be used as the care planning and management process

- specialist staff from learning disability services should provide support and advice to staff in mainstream community services, reducing the likelihood for admission

- there should be access to a local specialist in-patient unit, for those unable to use mainstream units.

The major government policy relating to mental health in England is the National Service Framework (NSF) for Mental Health (Department of Health, 1999). The NSF is applicable to all adults of working age, and this includes adults with learning disabilities. The NSF sets out seven standards that aim to improve the delivery of mental health care and reduce inequality, as follows:

- **Standard One**

  To ensure health and social services promote mental health and reduce the discrimination and social exclusion associated with mental health problems.

- **Standards Two and Three**

  To deliver better primary mental health care, and to ensure consistent advice and help for people with mental health needs, including primary care services for individuals with severe mental illness.

- **Standards Four and Five**

  To ensure that each person with a severe mental illness receives the range of mental health services they need; that crises are anticipated or prevented where possible; to ensure prompt and effective help if a crisis does occur; and timely access to an appropriate and safe mental health place or hospital bed, including a secure bed, as close to home as possible.

- **Standard Six**

  To ensure that health and social services assess the needs of carers who provide regular and substantial care for those with severe mental illness, and provide care to meet their needs.

- **Standard Seven**

  To ensure that health and social services play their full part in the achievement of the target in *Saving Lives: Our Healthier Nation* to reduce the suicide rate by at least one fifth by 2010.

More recently, the Foundation for People with Learning Disabilities, Valuing People Support Team and National Institute for Mental Health in England (NIMHE) (2004) produced *Green Light for Mental Health: How good are your mental health services for people with learning disabilities?* This document is principally an audit tool to enable local areas to improve their mental health support services for people with learning disabilities. *Green Light* also suggests ways in which the NSF for Mental Health standards can be achieved for people with learning disabilities.

Service models

There are three main service models that are employed to meet the mental health needs of people with learning disabilities. The amount and type of these services vary greatly across the UK, and some areas may adopt a multi-model approach, utilising aspects of several models.

1. Community learning disability services

Community learning disability teams (CLDTs) began to emerge in the 1980s as the hospital closure programme started to gain pace. Their role is to provide specialist health and social care packages for people with learning disabilities. They are multidisciplinary teams consisting of professionals from the local social services and primary care NHS trust, and often the mental health trust. Professionals will normally include social workers (or care managers), community learning disability nurses, clinical psychologists, occupational therapists, speech and language therapists and physiotherapists. Their role is beginning to change, as they take a more advisory and supporting role, working in collaboration with mainstream services (Department of Health, 2001).

In areas where a specialist mental health service for people with learning disabilities does not exist, CLDTs will commonly have a consultant psychiatrist within the team, and occasionally junior doctors. The psychiatrist will take a lead on the management of those people with mental health problems and contribute to the management of people whose behaviour is challenging. Some CLDTs will have a dedicated community nurse to provide mental health care, and he or she may be learning disability trained or mental health trained (and preferably dual trained). Mental health is not the primary focus for CLDTs, as they aim to meet a wide range of needs, including improving service users' communication skills, increasing and maintaining independence and supporting individuals to live in their local communities.

2. Specialist mental health in learning disability services

Over the last ten years, specialist mental health in learning disability (MHiLD) services have started to emerge. Their primary focus is on meeting the mental health needs of people with learning disabilities. The need for such specialist services lies in the increased vulnerability of people with learning disabilities, who often present with complex needs, requiring highly skilled assessment and adapted therapeutic interventions. The MHiLD services are multidisciplinary and are not usually directly part of learning disability services; some of them sit within mainstream mental health services. They work closely with professionals from both learning disability and adult mental health services. This type of service is able to use the facilities of mainstream services, such as acute admission and medium stay in–patient beds and a variety of community resources.

The MHiLD service has two distinct but intertwined functions: clinical–related and service–related. On a clinical level, the service provides highly specialised psychiatric assessment to people with all degrees of learning disabilities. Individual intervention packages are developed using a bio/psycho/social approach. Assessment and treatment may be home–based or on an outpatient basis, depending on the needs of the individual.

On a service level, the service provides advice and support to other clinical services, such as when people with learning disabilities are admitted to mainstream facilities. Consultation and training is regularly provided to organisations providing direct care and support to the service user, be it private or voluntary residential, day services or employment and outreach services. The training centres on educating carers and support staff about the mental health needs of the person. This includes minimising distress, observing for signs and symptoms of psychiatric disorder, avoiding potential triggers for relapse and promoting positive mental health.

Bouras *et al* (2003) describe how these specialist teams differ from generic adult community mental health teams. The teams have clear definitions of their target groups, have a fixed capacity, professionals have specific roles and responsibilities with little conflict, and training and skill levels are high. Bateman & Tyrer (2004) argue that specialist mental health teams show more successful outcomes than generic services, that withdrawal from services is significantly reduced and that they can make specific links with allied services such as housing, social services, probation and forensic services, and other care providing organisations. The development of these services will provide people with learning disabilities with the specialist clinical input that their needs dictate, whilst remaining within the framework of mainstream services, thus enabling better communication and collaborative working.

3. Mainstream mental health services

The core of mainstream services across the UK are similar, with variation in size and quantity. Services are generally divided by those for different age groups and for people requiring community or in-patient intervention.

Mainstream services were originally set up at a time when they were distinct (institutionally-based) separate services for people with learning disabilities. It was uncommon for people with learning disabilities to access mainstream mental health services. Consequently, staff in these services have had very limited (if any) experience in providing care for this complex group. Now some people with learning disabilities are beginning to access mainstream mental health services, the training needs of the staff need to be addressed.

Adult mental health services

Community mental health teams (CMHT)

Each district within the UK has at least one CMHT. Access to the team is generally by referral from primary care services. The CMHT provides assessment and treatment to individuals whose mental health needs cannot be met by their general practitioner. The teams are multidisciplinary (psychiatrists, social workers, psychologists, community psychiatric nurses and occupational therapists) and are based at an accessible location in the community.

In-patient services (adult acute mental health units)

The vast majority of people with mental health problems receive treatment in the community. But for a small number of people, a period of admission may be required where they can receive assessment and treatment in a structured and safe environment with 24–hour professional support. These service users are more likely to have a psychotic condition and lack insight into their mental state. The *Mental Health Act* (1983) is commonly used in these instances.

Adult acute units serve adults of a working age and are often situated within a general hospital. They have approximately 15 to 20 beds. Consultant psychiatrists lead the clinical team, with input from occupational therapy and psychology. Registered mental health nurses manage the unit and care delivery on a day-to-day basis.

Assertive outreach teams

Assertive outreach teams provide a specialised service to people with severe mental health problems who are at risk of losing contact with services and of relapsing. These are multidisciplinary and work on a round the clock basis. Team members do not carry individual caseloads, but the whole team acts as the keyworker and provides intensive support to the individual.

Crisis resolution/home treatment teams

These teams support people to receive treatment in the community, with minimal disruption to their lives. They offer a rapid response to people who are in crisis, and operate 24 hours a day. They are mainly staffed by mental health nurses, with the support of psychiatrists.

Child and adolescent mental health services (CAMHS)

Each local area has at least one CAMHS team working in the community. The team will consist of various disciplines including psychiatrists, psychologists, community psychiatric nurses and occupational therapists. They provide comprehensive assessment and treatment to children with mental health problems and behavioural disorders. CAMHSs emphasise early intervention to prevent or ameliorate the development of serious mental health problems, improve the mental health of children who are in care, offer support to families at risk of breakdown and aim to reduce school exclusion (Department of Health, 2002). Each area will have an in-patient unit for children and adolescents, or access to beds.

The Foundation for People with Learning Disabilities (2003) held an inquiry into the mental health needs of young people with learning disabilities. A key recommendation from the inquiry reinforced *Valuing People*'s theme of inclusion: mainstream mental health services for children and adolescents should develop the resources and expertise necessary to respond to young people with learning disabilities, their families and networks, and should not exclude people because they have learning disabilities.

Older persons mental health teams

Each district has a community team and in-patient service for people over the age of 65 who have mental health problems. The teams are multidisciplinary and work closely with general health services, due to the increased rates of physical ill health.

Forensic services

These are teams for people with mental health problems who have committed offences or are at risk of committing offences.

Discussion

People with learning disabilities should expect the same standard of mental health care as the rest of the population, but which model is best suited to do this is a matter of discussion.

Service users were thoroughly consulted when current policy was developed, and an emerging theme was that people with learning disabilities wanted the same right of access to mainstream health services as the rest of the population (Department of Health, 2001). The Tuesday Group (a mental health promotion group in south east London) stated that people with learning disabilities should use the same mental health services as everyone else, but staff should remember that they might need more support (Carter *et al*, 2004). However, it is not clear whether those consulted were basing their opinions on actual experience or on ideals. There is some evidence that some people with learning disabilities who have accessed mainstream in-patient services found the experience frightening and bewildering (Lynggaard *et al*, 2004).

Government policy is for people with learning disabilities to access mainstream mental health services whenever possible. It is recognised that, for this to happen, support from specialist services may be required, and that for some a specialist in-patient resource is needed.

Spiller *et al* (2004) examined the interface between specialist MHiLD and mainstream adult mental health acute wards. Mainstream staff stated that they had a lack of training, skills and experience in the area of mental health problems and people with learning disabilities. The majority believed that service users' needs would be best met on a specialist unit, due to their increased vulnerability, the negative attitudes of service users without learning disabilities and insufficient staff time to meet their different and increased needs. People with learning disabilities often require a longer period of admission (Bouras & Holt, 2004). This may contribute to the negativity of mainstream staff, as services are under continual pressure with sparse resources.

The *Green Light* toolkit (Foundation for People with Learning Disabilities, 2004) offers some ideas for overcoming these issues. It advises services to develop joint training opportunities for mainstream and learning disability staff, the development of joint working protocols with clear referral routes and the employment of liaison staff especially dedicated to improving the care pathway into mainstream services.

A possible solution to these difficulties is the specialisation of mental health services for people with learning disabilities provided by mainstream mental health services at a tertiary level (Bouras & Holt, 2004). It is a model that has proved successful for many other minority groups who present with complex needs (eg older people, people who misuse substances and those with offending behaviour), as specialist mental health teams have begun to emerge.

Conclusions

Mental health care for people with learning disabilities remains a relatively new concept and services are still in their infancy. Recent Government policy has seen a major change in direction of mental health services for people with learning disabilities, with very little being based on evidence. There is a risk that the mental health of people with learning disabilities will be dictated by ideology and the much-needed, evidence-based practice will be secondary.

References and further reading

Bateman AW & Tyrer P (2004) Services for people with personality disorder: organisation for inclusion. *Advances in Psychiatric Treatment* 10, 425–433.

Bouras N, Cowley A, Holt G, Newton JT & Sturmey P (2003) Referral trends of people with intellectual disabilities and psychiatric disorders. *Journal of Intellectual Disability Research* **47** (6) 439–446.

Bouras N & Holt G (2001) Community mental health services for adults with learning disabilities. In: G Thornicroft and G Szmukler (Eds) *Textbook of Community Psychiatry*. Oxford: Oxford University Press.

Bouras N & Holt G (2004) Mental health services for adults with learning disabilities. *British Journal of Psychiatry* 184, 291–292.

Carter J, Cronin P, Essam V, Hardy S, Hobbs T, Hope L, Montgomery Y, Peyton L, Smoker J, Stennet B, Woodward P & Zimmock Y (2004) *Our mental health*. Living Well **4** (2) 27–30.

Department of Health (1999) *Mental Health: National Service Framework*. London: HMSO.

Department of Health (2001) *Valuing People: A New Strategy for Learning Disability for the 21st Century*. London: HMSO.

Department of Health (2002) *What's new: Learning from the CAMHS Innovation projects*. London: HMSO.

Department of Health and Social Security (2004) *Equal Lives: Review of policy and services for people with a learning disability in Northern Ireland*. London: HMSO.

Foundation for People with Learning Disabilities (2003) *Count us in: The report of the committee of inquiry into meeting the mental health needs of young people with learning disabilities*. London: Foundation for People with Learning Disabilities.

Foundation for People with Learning Disabilities, Valuing People Support Team & National Institute for Mental Health in England (2004) *Green Light: How good are your mental health services for people with learning disabilities? A service improvement toolkit*. London: Foundation for People with Learning Disabilities.

Lynggaard H, Parkes C, Dutton S, Hall I & Hassiotis A (2004) The experience of people with intellectual disabilities using mainstream psychiatric services. *Journal of Intellectual Disability Research* 48, parts 4 & 5, 307.

Scottish Executive (2000) *The Same As You: A review of services for people with learning disability*. Scottish Executive.

Spiller M, Holt G, Bouras N, Whelan P, Al-Sheikh A, Marjanovic K, Faulkner A & Jones M (2004) *A qualitative contextual and strategic study of the operational interface between the specialist Mental Health in Learning Disabilities team and generic acute Adult Mental Health wards using the Framework methodology*. London: The Estia Centre.

Welsh Office (2001) *Fulfilling the Promises*. Welsh Office.

CHAPTER **SEVEN**

Challenging behaviour

THERESA JOYCE, GERVASE NEWRICK, DAN GEER AND JIM MOLLOY

Introduction

The term 'challenging behaviour' came into use in the 1980s, when major efforts were being made to close long-stay institutions. This was a time when services in the UK were increasingly being planned on the basis of how to implement the values and philosophy encapsulated in the term 'normalisation', as opposed to the previous situation where many of the aims of services seemed apparently more to do with containment and removal from society. Previously, people had been seen as having 'difficult' or 'problem' behaviour, or as being, of themselves, 'difficult' or 'problems'. In that sense, the individuals themselves 'took the blame' for the behaviour. The term 'challenging behaviour' was coined in an effort to redress this balance. Rather than the problem residing in the person, it was instead seen as a challenge for services to overcome.

Recognising and defining challenging behaviour

The challenge is in the nature of the service being able to meet effectively the needs of such individuals. It was recognised that people with learning disabilities would still engage in behaviours which were problematic for themselves or for those around them. Transfer to a community setting, such as a staffed house, would not, of itself, 'cure' problems, although it would hopefully reduce them. It is clear that real progress has been made in the ability of services to understand and respond to service users with challenging behaviour. There is now much greater capacity to deliver services in ways which really address the needs of service users with challenging behaviour – both by reducing the extent of such behaviour and/or by ensuring it can be managed if it cannot be 'cured'. Such placements also pay attention to the needs of service users to participate in activities inside and outside their home and thus focus on more than the challenging behaviour – they also focus on the rest of the service user's life. The challenge, therefore, is to respond effectively to service user's behaviour and to ensure that individuals have a good quality of life.

So, how do we define challenging behaviour in the circumstances of present-day services? The definition of challenging behaviour is complex. There is no single definition which clearly states and operationalises what is meant by challenging behaviour in a way that makes sense to all those who work with people who challenge. Emerson (1995) provides us with a definition, which is widely used:

> '*Culturally abnormal behaviour of such an intensity, frequency or duration that the physical safety of the person or others is likely to be placed in serious jeopardy, or behaviour which is likely to seriously limit use of, or result in the person being denied access to ordinary community facilities.*'

Notice how this definition encompasses the potential impact of behaviour on other individuals, the environment and the service user's lifestyle, and therefore reflects the ethos of many service philosophies; namely that people with learning disabilities should be supported to live as ordinary life as possible within the community and how the presence of challenging behaviour may limit this realisation (Blunden & Allen, 1990). It is therefore for service organisations to support people with learning disabilities in such a way as to maximise the individual's potential whilst acknowledging the risks and benefits of community living for that person.

However, this definition does not tell us how frequent, intense or long lasting the behaviour needs to be, or how much it should restrict access before it can be accurately labelled as challenging. This is because the behaviour inevitably occurs in a social context, and different settings have different levels of capacity to deal with, and tolerance to cope with, behaviour. Some behaviour may be deemed more or less challenging, dependent on the social situation in which it occurs and the staff's or service's ability to cope with the behaviour. Therefore, there can be wide variation in how much services are actually challenged by behavioural problems.

Research examining the prevalence of challenging behaviour has encountered difficulties in definition because of the differing social contexts in which challenging behaviour occurs. However, there is a consensus on the sorts of behaviour that pose a management problem, and the following behaviours were identified in people with learning disabilities in the north west of England by Emerson *et al* (1987).

Severely challenging behaviours include:

- non-compliance
- hair pulling, self and others
- smearing faeces
- verbal aggression
- pica (eating inedible objects)
- stripping in public
- absconding
- inappropriate sexual behaviour
- skin picking
- hitting others
- destructive behaviours
- screaming
- self-injury
- temper tantrums
- scratching, self and others
- theft.

Moderately challenging behaviours may feature:

- overactivity
- repetitive pestering
- disturbing noises
- regurgitating food
- self-induced vomiting
- stereotypied behaviour
- stuffing fingers in body openings.

The extent to which many of these types of behavioural problem may have an impact on services or the amount of community access an individual has, will depend on the frequency, intensity and duration of that behaviour. For example, an individual who screams once or twice an hour may still experience a full life in the community with support, whereas a service user who is frequently aggressive towards staff may be avoided. This may be due to the risk of injury and potential stresses experienced by support staff, and therefore experiences and opportunities for that individual could be seriously limited.

There is increasing evidence that good management and staff support is crucial if staff are to be enabled to work effectively with service users who present with behavioural problems. The ability of a service to provide appropriate support to service users with challenging behaviour will depend on a number of factors. These include many of the features outlined in the Mansell Report (Department of Health, 1993), which suggested that the competence of staff, the commitment of managers, support from specialist staff and good commissioning arrangements are crucial in providing effective services. These attributes would produce staff teams skilled in understanding and responding to challenging behaviour, and managers who provide the necessary support to enable them to do so.

Why does challenging behaviour occur?

Historically, people with learning disabilities were viewed as being almost predisposed to displaying difficult behaviour and that, by virtue of their learning disabilities, it was almost expected. In this way, challenging behaviour was considered part of an individual's make-up and therefore behavioural problems were not open to remediation. This view of challenging behaviour dominated for many years, until the advent of deinstitutionalisation, which focused attention on challenging behaviour in a way which recognised both the needs of the individual and the complexity of the possible causes of behaviour. There is now an orientation which assumes that there is a cause for the behaviour and that it is therefore explicable – it is not necessarily random or incomprehensible, or purposely aimed at staff. There has been a move away from medical/biological explanations for challenging behaviour, to an explanation which emphasises its social construction. In other words, challenging behaviour is a product of individual factors and the circumstances in which the individual lives, or has lived. It is therefore useful to consider a number of different factors in developing an understanding of challenging behaviour.

Biological causes of challenging behaviour

There are a selected number of syndromes, some of them genetically determined, which predispose an individual to display challenging behaviour, sometimes of a very specific type. However, these syndromes are extremely rare and many of the people with challenging behaviour encountered by staff are unlikely to fall into this category (Murphy, 1994).

Among the more well know syndromes are Lesch–Nyhan (characterised by self-injurious behaviour), Prader–Willi (with overeating, and aggression sometimes displayed when the person may be prevented from eating) and phenylketonuria (characterised by aggression, screaming, self-biting and kicking).

Increased understanding of both learning disabilities and behaviour has produced a less all-inclusive assessment of the likely impact of biological causes on challenging behaviour and, rather, biological factors should be thought of as a cause to eliminate through the process of assessment.

There is a link between epilepsy and challenging behaviour, particularly with frontal lobe epilepsy, which can cause aggressive behaviour and disinhibited sexualised behaviour. There is also a suggestion of a link between autism and challenging behaviour, although the nature of the link is not clear and there are equally powerful explanations which encompass issues to do with learned behaviour, communication and environmental causes.

Challenging behaviour can, however, have a physical cause. It can be caused by pain, or it can follow illness. For example, persistent pain could lead to self-injury, making noises or aggression; while the consequence of illness could be refusal to participate in activities, withdrawal and so on. This could occur due to fatigue as much as any other cause.

Challenging behaviour as a response to a poor environment

For many individuals, life in the community could all too easily resemble life back on the ward. People with challenging behaviour are most at risk of ending up in the poorest quality environments. They are known to be the most likely to be admitted and re-admitted to hospital, and the opportunities for participating in a range of activities are usually restricted for them. Their history, therefore, and (in some cases) present treatment can be characterised by a barren environment with few materials and activities, low levels of social interaction, and those interactions being negative and demanding rather than positive and supportive.

Such settings also often ignore all behaviour apart from 'problems', create the possibility of abuse and neglect, and restrict access to many things which are important for quality of life (for example, food and activity).

It is clear that the possibilities for developing and increasing behaviours which meet the need for interaction, for food and activity, for stimulation and for the avoidance of unpleasant demands, are much greater in these circumstances than in the circumstances of a responsive environment which is geared to providing for a whole range of needs (McGill & Toogood, 1993).

Challenging behaviour as learned behaviour

Challenging behaviour can be learned in the same way as any other behaviour can be learned: by the presentation of rewards following the behaviour. The behaviour may not, initially, occur with the intention of gaining a reward, but if an individual engages in behaviour and there is a consequence which they find pleasant, then they will eventually learn to pair behaviour with a consequence. Similarly, if the consequence is punishing, then the assumption is that eventually the behaviour will disappear.

There are two ways in which behaviour can be rewarded. The first is by positive reinforcement (ie something good/rewarding is given) and the second is by negative reinforcement (ie something unpleasant is removed).

The assumption behind the theory of learned behaviour is that new or old behaviours are developed and maintained through a process of association. The individual learns that the production of a particular behaviour produces positive consequences – either something stimulating or rewarding is delivered after the behaviour occurs, or something unpleasant is taken away. This process of behaviour and reward increases the likelihood of a behaviour re-occurring under the same conditions or circumstances. The things which can be defined as reinforcing will vary according to the individual's preferences. For example, cigarette smoking can be a very rewarding activity for one person and totally aversive for another. It is also likely that behaviours will occur in a given context under certain conditions, which can act as a precursor for the behaviour. Hence, staff are often asked to record much more than the occurrence of behaviour but everything that was going on at the time.

However, understanding what the behaviour achieves for the person and understanding the circumstances which make it more likely to occur, is a complex process, and requires careful assessment.

Historically, challenging behaviour was often labelled as 'attention-seeking' behaviour and dismissed for that very reason, or judged to be a random act. This overly simplistic view ignored a person's motivation to display challenging behaviour. It may be that behavioural problems are reinforced by attention, but the question is what is it about that attention that the person finds rewarding? It may be that a member of staff talks to the person, holds their hand or is more likely to offer the person something which they find interesting. The underlying assumption that people with learning disabilities should not be seeking attention was usually not acknowledged.

There is now a broad evidence base that there may be a range of 'types' of reward which behaviour may elicit. These are broadly categorised as:

- **social** – the reward is interaction with someone else
- **tangible** – the reward is something which can be touched, for example, food or drink

- **sensory** – the reward is sensory stimulation

- **demand avoidance** – the reward is that the requirement to do something difficult/unpleasant goes away

- **social escape** – the reward is getting away from a social situation the person finds unable to deal with.

(Emerson *et al*, 1987)

Challenging behaviour as a communicative act

Challenging behaviour can be seen as a way to communicate a need or to indicate refusal or distress, where the individual finds usual methods of communication difficult, if not impossible. In essence, the greater the difficulty the person has in communicating their message, the greater the likelihood that challenging behaviour will occur. Where an individual lacks a conventional method of communicating their message, they will adopt another way of relaying what it is they 'want to say'. There is now a widely accepted hypothesis that challenging behaviour is functional for individuals, and that it is possible to determine what meaning behaviour carries, by means of analysis.

Staff and other people who are familiar with the person with learning disabilities will often attempt to interpret the meaning of challenging behaviour. This is true whether or not the individual is intentionally trying to communicate with another person. (The individual may be reacting to an internal state, and might have no intention of communicating a message to another person.) However, if the challenging behaviour brings about a response from other people that does meet the individual's (possibly unidentified) need, then that individual might well use it again to get the same response, and indeed might generalise it to other circumstances in the hope that the same rewarding consequences occur.

This is why many treatment strategies for challenging behaviour involve teaching the individual alternative, more cost-effective methods of communicating their needs or their desire for a certain reward.

In essence, challenging behaviour can be seen as a way for people with learning disabilities to establish some control over a situation, or within an environment that they find difficult to deal with, or where their needs are not fully met.

Challenging behaviour as a response to emotional trauma

People with learning disabilities are subject to a range of responses from those around them, some of which may be supportive and some of which may be abusive. The abuse can be physical, sexual, financial or emotional, and all of these will have an effect on the individual. It is now also recognised that people can and do find their disabilities painful to cope with (Sinason, 1992). Some challenging behaviours can be traced back to situations in which the individual has been abused, and it is useful to remember that verbal abuse (for example, name-calling and being laughed at) is not an uncommon experience for people with learning disabilities. It is also important to remember that people with learning disabilities are vulnerable to sexual abuse (Turk & Brown, 1993), and challenging behaviour can be a response to this trauma.

Challenging behaviour can also be an expression of a person's anger, misery or pain at the fact that they are disabled, and the life experiences to which this has led.

Challenging behaviour in relation to a mental illness

People with learning disabilities are susceptible to problems with mental health just like any other individual from the general population, and this can affect their behaviour. So, during the assessment phase, it is important to exclude diagnosable mental illness as a cause of challenging behaviour.

Assessing the causes of challenging behaviour

The previous section outlined possible causes of challenging behaviour. This section will consider how to assess those causes – it is clear that there is unlikely to be one simple 'cause'.

In order to assess behaviour, we must clearly define the behaviour or behaviours that we are interested in. It is not sufficient simply to label behaviour as 'aggression' or 'self-injury', as this does not describe accurately what the behaviour looks like. Rather, the behaviour must be defined in very concrete terms, and we call this 'topography'. When defining behaviour in preparation for measurement, it is useful to ask ourselves whether two people observing the behaviour would define it as the same thing. Different behaviours may have the same function and the same behaviour can have different functions. For example, one service user frequently used self-injury in order to obtain a cup of tea. However, occasionally she also used self-injury in order to be removed from an environment which she found to be too noisy.

A full analysis nevertheless requires much more than noting when the behaviour occurs. Many individuals have more than one challenging behaviour, and each behaviour needs to be analysed and considered separately.

The main methods of assessing challenging behaviour have a number of components. They require examination of the individual's history, especially in terms of previous interventions and placements; this helps to determine if previous environments may have played a part in the development of the behaviour. Assessment of the environment is important (for example, in terms of routines, activities, staff and other service users), as is assessment of the target behaviours, both in terms of antecedents and consequences. Assessment must be a holistic process, taking into account all that is known about a person and all that surrounds them. It is also important to assess reinforcers or rewards for the individual. This can be done, for example, with the help of an instrument such as the *Reinforcement Inventory for Adults* (Willis & LaVigna, 1985).

This type of comprehensive assessment is often called functional analysis, as it implies that not only is the behaviour assessed, but also as many as possible of the variables or factors which might contribute to it. In other words, we are seeking to discover what purpose behaviour serves for that specific person. It is essentially an individualistic approach, and requires careful observation and good knowledge of the individual and his or her life.

Functional analysis is, therefore, much more complex than the sorts of assessment which were once routinely undertaken. Staff will be asked to keep records, but these are unlikely to be the main or sole source of information about the circumstances in which the challenging behaviour occurs. Analysis of challenging behaviour should no longer be based simply on ABC charts (antecedent, behaviour and consequence), although such information will still be necessary.

A number of structured instruments are now available to gather relevant information. One example of such instruments is the *Behaviour Assessment Guide* (Willis *et al*, 1987).

Assessment also requires observation. This is increasingly being carried out with the aid of microcomputers programmed so that observed behaviour can be categorised according to the type of behaviour that is occurring.

Non-aversive intervention

Following a detailed assessment of challenging behaviour, an intervention plan needs to be devised which will address what is to be done to reduce problem behaviour. In this section, we will look at a basic intervention model comprised of four interrelated components, none of which should be implemented in isolation. These four elements form the basis of the intervention plan, which should be devised in line with the individual's wishes, aspirations and known preferences. The most recent 'person–centred planning' meeting and previous documents should provide valuable information to inform the development of the intervention plan.

In this brief section, it is not possible to go into the intricacies of developing complex behavioural programmes but, by the end of this chapter, readers will be able to effect positive change for their service users in the way their needs are met and in the way they are supported.

The intervention model

The four elements to intervention are:

- teaching new behaviours
- changing the environment
- focused behavioural support
- responding to challenging behaviour.

Each of these components will be discussed in detail.

Teaching new behaviours

The dominance of the medical model in the treatment of challenging behaviour and people with learning disabilities meant that treatment once tended to focus on the eradication of problem behaviour by the use of many unethical and punishing procedures. The modern intervention approach for challenging behaviour is termed 'positive behavioural support'. This model is not only concerned with the use of behavioural method but also with social inclusion and community integration. In any intervention, these aspects are included and measured in terms of positive changes in quality of life in establishing the positive outcomes of intervention.

Following assessment, a clear function(s) for the behaviour will have been identified and the aim of intervention will be to find a 'functionally equivalent' behaviour that the individual can use instead of challenging behaviour, to achieve the same

Mental Health in Learning Disabilities **A reader** © Pavilion Publishing (Brighton) Ltd 2005

aim or reward. Therefore, if an individual screams loudly to escape social situations or when they are approached, it would be logical to teach an alternative method to communicate the message 'I want you to go away'. This could entail holding up a square of coloured card to indicate this instead of screaming, or by using a simple gesture or Makaton sign. It must be borne in mind, however, that the new behaviour needs to be as (or more) effective than the challenging behaviour, and easy to produce.

In addition to teaching alternative behaviours, it may also be advantageous to teach new skills to the people we work with. Staying with the above example, we could help our service user to feel more relaxed in a social situation either by teaching a relaxation method or by enabling them to communicate about a topic or their day with staff or other service users. This may help to make social situations less aversive and may, in time, reduce the likelihood of screaming occurring. When considering teaching alternative behaviours or new skills, it is important to make a judgement about whether the person is able to learn this new behaviour. Questions to bear in mind are:

- Does the person already perform similar behaviours?
- Are they physically able?
- Will they be motivated to learn this skill?
- If not, how can we motivate or reward them for learning?

Given the abilities of some of the people we work with, it would be easy to be over-zealous in the teaching of new skills, and service users could be on permanent training programmes. Therefore it is important that any considerations to teach new skills are based on an individual's level of need, because it may take considerable time and effort on their behalf to achieve the aim.

Changing the environment

There is now a body of knowledge about how we can organise environments so that at least some of the features implicated in the production of challenging behaviour can be addressed. McGill and Toogood (1994) provide a summary of the way in which characteristics of the environment can maintain challenging behaviour, and point out which features should be present in high-quality services, which will work to reduce challenging behaviour.

Behaviour maintained by:	Environment characterised by:
Escape or avoidance of aversive situations	Intermittently high levels of overt and covert social control and abuse
Increased social contact	Low levels of social contact
Adjustment of levels of sensory stimulation	Barren, unstimulating environment
Increased access to preferred objects and activities(tangible reinforcement)	Regimes which rigidly control access to preferred objects/activities

From *Providing Helpful Environments* (McGill & Toogood, 1993)

This summary of the way in which environments can actually mediate the production of challenging behaviour provides clear direction for the way in which environments can be helpful. There need to be:

- good levels of positive interaction, which can be based around appropriate rather than inappropriate behaviour

- staff support to participate in activities

- a range of activities and materials which are relevant and meaningful.

Clearly, this all needs organisation and management. It is not helpful if activities occur on an ad hoc or unpredictable basis, and if the support to participate in them is inconsistent. Service users and staff need to know what they should be doing, when they should be doing it and with whom, to ensure that opportunities and support to take part in them are consistent and predictable. Ensuring that this information is communicated effectively to service users will mean employing a number of different methods to get the messages across. These will include the use of visual timetables, communication books, object cues and perhaps object cue timetables. In terms of staff, sharing their time effectively between residents will need to be worked out carefully, with the aid of shift planning and the allocation of specific duties.

Attention can also be paid to possible triggers for behaviour in the environment and action taken to reduce them. Take, for example, high levels of noise. How many times have there been situations where people are talking, the television is on, the radio is on in another room, and the washing machine is on? The aim is to produce an environment in which constructive activity is planned and available, and in which inappropriate behaviour can be replaced, over time, with more appropriate alternatives.

Focused behavioural support

Prior to the growth of behaviour analysis, the 'treatment' for challenging behaviour was behaviour modification. Many of the responses to the behaviour were 'punishing', the assumption being that if the consequences for the service user were 'unpleasant' then the behaviour would be suppressed. However, in the absence of a sophisticated understanding of what each individual found rewarding or punishing, and in the absence of an understanding of the function of the behaviour, many staff working with people with challenging behaviour adopted simplistic solutions to all behaviour. Behaviour was therefore often described as 'attention-seeking' and the response was to ignore it. This was based on the assumption that if the behaviour was not rewarded it would disappear. Sometimes, more active strategies were used. For example, the response to aggression was often time-out or seclusion. This would have a punishing effect if the function of the behaviour was to get attention. If the function of the behaviour was to avoid an activity or a situation, however, then time-out (by removing the demand) would actually reinforce the behaviour.

Reinforcement can be delivered in a manner which develops more appropriate behaviours, either by reinforcing the non-occurrence of the challenging behaviour and/or by reinforcing other, more appropriate behaviours. For example, if an individual challenges services by screaming, then staff can deliver reinforcement for specific periods of time when screaming does not occur; they can deliver reinforcement when appropriate language or communication occurs; and they can try to teach more appropriate methods of communicating the need presently being expressed by screaming.

In addition to using reinforcement as a means of helping people develop more appropriate behaviours, individuals with challenging behaviour may also find that being taught to relax in stressful situations or when they get anxious is useful. A psychotherapeutic approach can also be useful in terms of being able to help individuals cope with the pain of their disability.

Responding to challenging behaviour

As well as providing a helpful environment, teaching new skills and structuring reinforcement to help replace behaviours, staff also need to know how to respond when the behaviour does occur. Challenging behaviour does not disappear overnight and, in many cases, does not completely disappear at all. There needs to be a clearly worked out strategy for what people should do when challenging behaviour does occur. This is necessary to keep the service users, staff and members of the public safe. People will need to know how to diffuse the situation quickly and safely in a way that does not antagonise the person further. This may mean employing strategies in distraction, interruption or instructional control, or making very sudden changes to the mood of the environment, perhaps by doing something silly such as singing, dancing or playing music, or by removing the individual from the setting and going for a walk. When responding to challenging behaviour, the aim is to stop the behaviour. At this stage, you should not be thinking about how your responses may reinforce the behaviour, or thinking, 'if I do this they will just get what they want'. In essence, reactive management should be carefully worked out and everybody should be well-versed in its use. Giving PRN medication (as required) might also be part of a reactive strategy, as might breakaway and/or control and restraint procedures (although hopefully not frequently). If restraint procedures are to be used, then all staff need to be trained in them by an instructor qualified to do so, and the procedures need to be regularly reviewed and monitored.

Reactive management strategies also need to be worked out with staff on a very individual basis, taking service user behaviour and staff skills and competencies into account.

Conclusion

In this chapter, we have looked at the various causes of challenging behaviour and how these may be formed and maintained by previous learning and conditions within the environment and by the presence of physical ill health. In understanding the causes of challenging behaviour, it will always be necessary to conduct a full functional assessment, taking into account all that is known about a person, to determine the meaning of the problem behaviour.

Once functional analysis is complete, it will be possible to design an intervention plan comprising four components: teaching new skills; changing the environment; focused behavioural support; and responding to challenging behaviours. The plan should be based on the individual's known preferences and aspirations, and should have the aims of social inclusion and the improvement of quality of life at its core.

References and further reading

Blunden R & Allen D (Eds) (1990) *Facing the challenge: An ordinary life for people with learning difficulties and challenging behaviour.* London: Kings Fund.

Department of Health (1993) *Services for People with Learning Disabilities and Challenging Behaviour or Mental Health Needs: Report of a Project Group* (Chair: Professor JL Mansell). London: HMSO.

Emerson E (1995) *Challenging Behaviour: Analysis and intervention in people with learning difficulties.* Cambridge: Cambridge University Press.

Emerson E, Barrett S, Bell C, Cummings R, McCool C & Toogood A (1987) *Developing Services for People with Severe Learning Difficulties and Challenging Behaviours.* Canterbury: Institute of Social and Applied Psychology, University of Kent.

Felce D & Lowe K (1993) Supporting people with severe learning difficulties and challenging behaviour in ordinary housing. In: Kiernan C (Ed) *Research to Practice? Implications of research on the challenging behaviour of people with learning disability.* Kidderminster: British Institute of Learning Disabilities.

Iwata B, Dorsey M, Slifer K, Bauman K & Richman G. (1982) Towards a functional analysis of self-injury. *Analysis and Intervention in Developmental Disabilities* 2, 3–20.

King TM (1995) *Reactive Management Strategies.* London: Lewisham and Guy's Mental Health NHS Trust.

McGill P & Toogood A (1993) Providing helpful environments. In: E Emerson, P McGill and J Mansell (Eds.) *Severe Learning Disabilities and Challenging Behaviours – Designing high quality services.* London: Chapman and Hall.

Murphy G (1994) Understanding challenging behaviour. In: E Emerson, P McGill and J Mansell (Eds.) *Severe Learning Disabilities and Challenging Behaviours – Designing high quality services.* London: Chapman and Hall.

Sinason V (1992) *Mental Handicap and Human Condition: New approaches from the Tavistock.* London: Free Association Books.

Slater E & Roth M (1969) Mental subnormality. *Clinical Psychiatry* 692–735. London: Bailliere, Tindall and Cassell.

Turk V & Brown H (1993) Sexual abuse of adults with a learning disability: Results of a two-year incidence survey. *Mental Handicap Research* 6, 193–216.

Willis T, La Vigna G & Donnellan A (1987) *Behaviour Assessment Guide.* California: Institute for Applied Behaviour Analysis.

Willis T & La Vigna G (1985) *Reinforcement Inventory for Adults.* California: Institute for Applied Behaviour Analysis.

CHAPTER EIGHT

Epilepsy

ROBERT WINTERHALDER AND COLIN HEMMINGS

Introduction

This chapter gives a summary of epilepsy: the definition, prevalence, classification, causes, impact, diagnosis and alternative diagnoses, association with psychiatric disorders and some key service issues of epilepsy, with particular reference to people with learning disabilities. Management of epilepsy in people with learning disabilities will then be outlined.

What is epilepsy?

Epilepsy is a group of conditions in which people have a *tendency to have recurrent seizures*. *Seizures* are occasional, excessive and abnormal discharges of electrical activity in groups of brain cells that usually last for some seconds or minutes. Although the best-known type of seizure involves *convulsions*, seizures also manifest in other ways.

How common is epilepsy?

About 1 person in 150 has epilepsy at any one time. However, epilepsy is not always life-long and as people get older, their seizures may decrease or even cease. In contrast, others may develop seizures for the first time as they age, because of the onset of medical conditions such as stroke and dementia. People with epilepsy also have increased death rates at all ages. It has been estimated that 1 person in 30 will develop epilepsy at some point in their life.

Epilepsy and learning disabilities

Epilepsy is more common in people with learning disabilities, although still, most do not have it. When the level of learning disabilities is more severe, it is more likely that there will also be epilepsy. About 1 person in 20 with mild learning disabilities has epilepsy, rising to 1 in 2 in people with profound learning disabilities. Compared with people with epilepsy generally, people with epilepsy *and* learning disabilities tend to have increased frequency and mix of seizures; they are also more likely to have the types of seizure that can be difficult to treat.

What are the causes of epilepsy?

In the majority of people (around 70%), the exact original cause of epilepsy is unknown. In these cases, unidentified genetic factors may be important. A family history of epilepsy increases a person's chances of having it themselves; about 30% of people with epilepsy have a close relative with the condition. The most common known causes of epilepsy are those that have produced brain damage. In the newborn, birth injury (especially with lack of oxygen), structural malformations, metabolic disorders and infections such as meningitis are recognised causes. In the elderly, known causes of epilepsy are strokes and dementia. Other causes of epilepsy include head injury and brain tumours.

Even when the original cause is unknown, triggers for individual seizures can often be recognised. These include anxiety, over-excitedness, boredom, frustration, tiredness, alcohol, infections, low blood sugar, menstruation and certain medications. The seizure 'threshold' is reduced during sleep, so seizures often occur in the early hours.

How does epilepsy affect a person's life?

Having epilepsy reduces some people's confidence and self-esteem. They worry about the embarrassment of having seizures in public and this can lead to avoidance of situations and relationships. Some may be in denial of their epilepsy and may be non-compliant with treatment. People with epilepsy can still do work, courses, swimming and computing, and can still watch television, but they need to take care to reduce risks of having a seizure. A balance must be found between minimising the potentially adverse consequences of seizures and imposing unnecessary restrictions on the person. The person's family must be made aware of the risks, yet be discouraged from overprotecting their relative.

Seizures can have serious, even fatal consequences. They may worsen intellectual functioning by impairing attention, learning and memory. Recurrent severe and prolonged seizures may also cause further progressive brain damage, most probably by lack of oxygen or head injury. This can possibly further worsen seizure control and intellectual functioning. Epilepsy is sometimes caused by medical conditions that themselves increase the risk of death (such as brain tumours). Epilepsy can also be a cause of sudden death in its own right. This sometimes occurs as a result of respiratory problems or irregular heart rhythms during *status epilepticus*, an unusually prolonged single seizure or a rapid succession of brief repeated seizures lasting 30 minutes or longer. Deaths may also occur through accidents associated with seizures, such as head injuries and drowning.

Types of seizure

The classification by the International League Against Epilepsy is the one most used today. It classifies seizures into *simple* or *complex*, based on whether or not consciousness is unimpaired. Seizures are also divided into *partial* or *generalised*, depending on whether or not they begin in one particular region of the brain. Generalised seizures that begin as partial are referred to as *secondary generalised* seizures (rather than *primary generalised* seizures).

Simple partial seizures may cause motor symptoms such as twitching, or sensory symptoms such as tingling in one area of the body. *Complex partial* seizures usually originate in the temporal lobe of the brain. They cause impairment of consciousness, together with signs and symptoms as diverse as hallucinations, sudden strong emotions and automatisms. *Automatisms* are complex, semi–purposeful movements in impaired consciousness, such as lip smacking, chewing, swallowing and rubbing. An *aura* happens just before the main part of the seizure and is itself a partial seizure. Auras often originate in the temporal lobe and consist of a wide range of odd phenomena like a funny taste or smell, or a 'rising' sensation in the stomach. *Prodromal* symptoms sometime precede seizures and are different from auras. They can continue for hours or days and usually consist of changes in the person's mood, such as irritability or anxiety. They are ended by the seizure.

Generalised seizures are accompanied by impaired consciousness, and include atonic, myoclonic, absence and tonic–clonic types. They can be with a partial onset (secondary generalised) or without (primary generalised). *Atonic* seizures are also known as 'drop attacks' because they produce sudden loss of muscle tone and falls. *Myoclonic* seizures cause convulsions of a single limb. They are particularly associated with more severe learning disabilities. *Absence* seizures cause the person to look blank or vacant for a few seconds or minutes, but the person then often continues what they had been doing previously.

Tonic-clonic seizures are the most familiar type of generalised seizure, and consist of *tonic* and *clonic* phases. Sometimes people have seizures involving the tonic phase alone (*tonic* seizures). In the *tonic* phase, the person may suddenly let out a short cry due to muscular contraction, lose consciousness and fall to the ground. They may wet or soil themselves and bite their tongue or lips. They may become rigid and temporarily stop breathing. In a tonic–clonic seizure, after a short period of seconds following the tonic phase, the *clonic* phase begins, in which there are rapid alternate contractions and relaxations of muscles causing the body to rhythmically jerk (*convulsions*). Breathing may become noisy and irregular, and the person's jaw may be clenched.

Typically, after the clonic phase, the person remains unconscious for a few minutes. In the post-seizure (*post-ictal*) state a person may have a headache, be drowsy and want to sleep. Some people may instead be more irritable and confused.

How is epilepsy diagnosed?

The diagnosis of epilepsy is essentially 'clinical', made on history and observation. The person themselves often cannot remember their own seizures. That is why observations made by relatives and care staff are crucial. Often, the community learning disability nurse will work closely with the carers and doctor to ensure that the relevant information is obtained. Further assessments include mental state and physical examinations, and special investigations such as blood tests, brain scans and the electroencephalogram (EEG).

Special investigations are mainly done to confirm or refute the diagnosis and look for possible causes and triggers of seizures. However, they do have limitations, especially the EEG. A person with epilepsy may have a normal EEG result in between seizures and, rarely, a person without epilepsy may have an abnormal EEG result. Some service users will have difficulties in co-operating with various investigations. Functional behavioural analysis may also help to distinguish whether or not behaviours are mainly due to seizures, psychiatric illness, other factors or a combination of any or all of these. Investigation into the cause of the epilepsy is important, as it may discover a treatable condition and give information on its best treatment.

What other conditions can look like epilepsy?

There are many possible alternative diagnoses for what might appear to be seizures. These include various psychiatric disorders, migraines, irregular heart rhythms, strokes, 'pseudoseizures' and simple faints, as well as 'acute confusional states' due to causes such as low blood sugar, drug use, alcohol withdrawal and brain infections.

Information useful in distinguishing other disorders from epilepsy may be learned from the history. This should include symptoms before, during and after what appears to be a seizure, as well as its onset and duration. For example, in panic attacks the duration is usually longer than in a seizure, there may be over-breathing and there is no change in consciousness. *Pseudoseizures* look like seizures but there is no abnormal electrical discharge. They are not always consciously fabricated, and usually express psychological distress. Distinguishing pseudoseizures and epileptic seizures can be difficult, especially as a person may have both.

Simple violent outbursts may be wrongly viewed as epilepsy because during and immediately after some seizures people may act aggressively. Purposeful and motivated acts of violence associated with a seizure are rare.

Diagnosis of epilepsy in learning disabilities

Conclusive diagnosis of epilepsy can be difficult, and often even more so in people with learning disabilities. They may not be able to describe their experiences, or at least have limited vocabulary to do so. They are more likely to have stereotypies and medication-induced movement disorders, for example, head movements, rocking and jerking. They may show long-standing odd behaviours and neurological deficits. It may be difficult to distinguish impaired consciousness in the more severely disabled. To complicate matters further, seizures can affect people in different ways at different times.

Management

1. Medication used in the treatment of epilepsy (anticonvulsants)

Uses

The aim of therapy is to prevent seizures with as little medication as possible. Medication is generally started at a low dose and slowly increased to a dose which controls the epilepsy. Similarly, withdrawal of medication should be done gradually, for fear of a return of, or increase in, seizures. However, many of our service users have severe epilepsy, which necessitates the use of more than one drug. If more than one drug is used, the anticonvulsant drugs may interact with each other and alter the levels of drug in the body. This may lead to very high levels (toxicity) or very low (sub-therapeutic) levels, and reduced seizure control.

Blood monitoring

Blood tests are carried out for two main reasons. The first of these is to check the level of drug in the blood. Certain drugs are only effective at certain blood levels (for example, phenytoin) and blood tests can help to decide the dose of drug to be taken. Some drugs have side effects when the level of drug in the blood is too high. When epilepsy worsens, it may be wise to check the levels of anticonvulsants. With stable epilepsy, some doctors advise an annual check of blood levels. With the majority of drugs, it is not necessary to check the blood levels because they do not correspond to the effectiveness of the drug. The second reason for blood tests to be carried out is that drugs may have an effect on certain parts of the body, such as the liver, kidneys or blood, and the doctor may decide to order some blood tests to check that these are functioning correctly. Other indications for checking drug blood levels include concerns that the service user may not be taking the medication, or when several anticonvulsants have been prescribed, in order to help the doctor decide which drug needs to be adjusted.

Side effects

Many anticonvulsant drugs are sedative, which can lead to drowsiness and poor concentration. In people with learning disabilities, these drugs can further impair their ability to learn. phenytoin and phenobarbitone are the worst culprits, and most people have now been weaned off phenobarbitone and put on newer drugs. In the past few years, a number of new drugs – lamotrigine, vigabatrin, gabapentin, topiramate and levetiracetam – have become available. None of the anticonvulsant drugs are addictive, with the exception of the barbiturates (eg phenobarbitone) and the benzodiazepines (eg diazepam). Fortunately, phenobarbitone is no longer used as a mainstream anticonvulsant, and diazepam is only administered episodically, (eg when the service user is in status epilepticus) and therefore does not tend to lead to addiction and dependency.

2. Choice of anticonvulsant medication

Nowadays, service users presenting with epilepsy for the first time are no longer prescribed drugs such as phenobarbitone or phenytoin. However, people who have been stabilised on phenytoin and who are not experiencing any significant side effects, may continue to have this drug prescribed for them.

Currently, service users presenting with generalised seizures are prescribed either sodium valproate (Epilim) or lamotrigine (Lamictal) as the drugs of choice. For service users presenting with partial seizures, carbamazepine (Tegretol) in addition to either lamotrigine or sodium valproate are the drugs of first choice. If initial treatment fails, an add–on drug is chosen – levetiracetam has a good side effect profile and does not interact with other anticonvulsants; topiramate is also an effective anticonvulsant but may be second choice to levetiracetam because of concerns about possible cognitive difficulties. Other drugs that may be considered include gabapentin and tiagabine.

Rarely, but more so in people with learning disabilities because of the treatment-resistant nature of seizure disorders in this group, up to three anticonvulsants may need to be prescribed. Very occasionally, a long-term benzodiazepine such as clobazam may be considered when other options have failed.

Individuals who have epilepsy and learning disabilities often have a need for treatment for prolonged or cluster seizures – often, this is to prevent service users going into status epilepticus. Benzodiazepines tend to be the drug of choice – diazepam may be given orally or rectally, midazolam may be given intranasally or applied to the inside of the cheek, and so on. Such treatments require clear guidelines for their administration wherever possible. Residential providers should have a clear policy regarding the assessment of risk of their service users with epilepsy (see the section on service issues later in this chapter). Medication can be altered to overcome this. For example, women may experience increased seizures around menstruation and may need additional benzodiazepine medication during this phase.

3. Non-medical interventions

The physical environment of people with epilepsy must be as safe, but also as conducive to self-development and independence, as possible. Occasionally, it can be desirable for a person to carry an 'epilepsy' card or wear a protective helmet to reduce the risk of serious head injury. However, it must be remembered that such measures may increase stigma, and the wishes of the person with epilepsy should be considered wherever possible.

It is well recognised that increased stress levels may lead to deterioration in seizure control. Adverse environmental factors, together with psychological distress, may precipitate seizures. As in the general population, it is important for people with learning disabilities and epilepsy to maintain a stable lifestyle, which includes maintaining a regular sleep routine, not abusing alcohol or illicit drugs, avoiding excessive fatigue etc.

In addition to rectifying any environmental and/or psychological factors which may be contributing to poor seizure control, additional non–medical interventions can include relaxation therapy and aromatherapy. However, especially in the case of aromatherapy, the aromatherapist needs to be aware that certain oils can worsen seizure control. If in doubt, carers should discuss this with the service user's doctor.

Epilepsy and psychiatric disorders

People with epilepsy have a higher rate of psychiatric disorders than the general population. Rates of conditions such as depression are particularly high and are thought to be due to a combination of biological, psychological and social factors. Both epilepsy and learning disabilities are factors that are known to independently increase the chances of a person having psychiatric disorders and behavioural problems. Thus it would be expected that people who have both learning disabilities and epilepsy should be at an even greater risk of also having a psychiatric disorder. Whether or not this is actually the case remains unclear as yet.

In the post-seizure period, there may be a confusional state with psychotic symptoms such as delusional beliefs and hallucinations. Psychotic episodes and increased behavioural problems can occur in some people when their seizures are better controlled. However, they sometimes happen in others when their seizure control deteriorates. It has also become increasingly recognised that 'non-convulsive' type (absence and complex partial) status epilepticus can last for days or even weeks at a time, giving an abnormal mental state. Many people with more severe learning disabilities cannot verbalise distress, and so potentially may be showing problem behaviours in response to distressing experiences such as strange auras. Hence, whether any co-existing psychiatric symptoms or 'challenging behaviours' are directly due to seizures or whether they are unrelated, is inevitably complex.

Service issues (including risk policies)

The use of rectally administered diazepam (Stesolid) to bring seizures to an end and prevent status epilepticus and unnecessary admission to hospital should be addressed at an organisational level. It is essential that staff be given the opportunity to attend a training course in basic life-saving skills, including learning how to place someone in the recovery position after a seizure. Staff should also receive training in the administration of Stesolid. Clear policies and procedures should be in place.

All individuals with learning disabilities and epilepsy should have a risk assessment and management plan. For those service users living at home with their families, or living independently with minimal support, it is usually up to the medical team (consisting of doctors and nurses) to ensure that they have carried out an appropriate assessment. For those service users residing within the local authority or private/voluntary sector, the organisation should have a clear policy on epilepsy, which should include risk assessment, training, staff supervision etc. There should be clear protocols and guidelines and these should include when to seek further guidance and input from local health services – usually this will start with the service user's GP who may in turn refer on to the community learning disability team or neurology department.

A risk assessment should include any history of status or epilepsy-related injury, recent changes in medication, compliance issues, known triggers to seizures, levels of support during both the day and the night, risk situations both indoors and outdoors, and other issues such as driving, irregular lifestyle, contraception and pregnancy (in the case of women). All risk assessments must finish off with a management plan that includes identification of the risk, action to be taken and by whom, timescales and review dates.

Conclusion

Epilepsy is a serious neurological condition that can have a significant impact on an individual's functioning. Care staff have an important role to play in ensuring that people with learning disabilities and epilepsy received the best assessment, management and care available, thereby optimising their quality of life (see **Box 8.1** below).

Box 8.1: Role of carers

1. Make sure you have an understanding of the basic seizure types.

2. Record seizures accurately and have the information available for the doctor or nurse.

3. Support users with taking their medication and maintaining a healthy lifestyle.

4. Be aware of the main side effects of the anticonvulsants being prescribed.

5. Be aware (where relevant) of organisational risk assessment/management policies and procedures, and ensure that risk in the environment has been minimised.

6. Where relevant, ensure you have received adequate training regarding status epilepticus.

7. Promote positive attitudes towards people with learning disabilities.

References and further reading

Introductory level

Hanscomb A & Hughes L (2002) *Epilepsy*. London: Cassell Illustrated.

National Society for Epilepsy (1997) *Epileptic Seizures*. Chalfont St Peter: National Society for Epilepsy.

A variety of fact sheets and leaflets are available from the National Society for Epilepsy at www.epilepsynse.org.uk

Advanced level

Betts T (1998) *Epilepsy, Psychiatry and Learning Difficulty*. London: Taylor & Francis.

Trimble M (Ed) (2003) *Learning Disability and Epilepsy: An Integrative Approach*. Guildford: Clarius Press Ltd.

For service users

Band R (1998) *Epilepsy*. London: The Elfrida Society.

National Society for Epilepsy (2002) *About Epilepsy*. Chalfont St Peter: The National Society for Epilepsy.

Hollins S, Bernal J & Thacker A (1999) *Getting on with epilepsy*. London: Gaskell.

A variety of booklets is available from the Elfrida Society (including on EEG and MRI scan) at www.efrida.com

Useful contacts

The National Society for Epilepsy
Chalfont St Peter
Gerrards Cross
Bucks SL9 ORG
Tel: 01494 601300

CHAPTER NINE

Staff stress and coping strategies

JOHN ROSE, DAVID ROSE AND CHRIS HODGKINS

Introduction

Staff are at the front line of service delivery, and have a direct impact on the daily lives of people with learning disabilities. As staff are central to the delivery of services, they should be considered one of the most important assets, particularly as staff salaries constitute a significant part of service expenditure. As such, the quality of staff performance should be a prime concern in light of scarce resources.

Staff can experience poor morale and high stress, with up to a third reporting such high levels of stress that they are indicative of mental health problems (Hatton *et al*, 1999). Staff who are deemed to be highly stressed or burnt out are much more likely to give up their job or be absent due to sickness. This can have significant implications in terms of the high financial costs to the service providers of recruiting staff, but perhaps more importantly, to the loss of skilled staff providing the continuity of stable, high quality care to service users.

Stress can be particularly high in support staff in learning disability services, as they are often subject to considerable changes in roles and responsibilities since the introduction of community care and the reorganisation of the National Health Service (NHS). This has entailed considerable changes in roles, responsibilities and working practices, and has added to many staff members' feelings of insecurity.

While there are relatively few research findings about the relationship between stress and quality of care provided, some research evidence does suggest that staff who report lower levels of stress or strain do provide a better quality of care, particularly in terms of the type of interactions that they have with the people they work with. For example, Rose, Jones and Fletcher (1998) found that staff who reported lower levels of stress were shown to give residents more positive interactions and more assistance than that which would normally be observed when staff are trying to teach and develop skills in service users.

Stress – what is it?

The use of the term 'stress' is so common that defining it should not be difficult, but definitions of stress are as varied as the fields in which it has been investigated. Although a consensus definition of stress remains elusive, however, three common uses of the word continue to be used. Firstly, stress can refer to an internal state whereby a person may identify feeling unwell after working under pressure, and this is frequently labelled as 'strain'. Secondly, stress may refer to an external event whereby a person may deem feeling unwell or distressed as a direct consequence of workload pressures. This is often termed as a 'stressor'. Finally, stress may refer to a transactional process between environmental context and the individual. It is this use that has been a particular focus when considering occupational stress in staff working in learning disability services.

Many psychological descriptions of stress include not only a notion of demand being placed on an individual but also something about the way that individual looks at or appraises a demand, and how this relates to their perceived ability to cope. Stress is represented internally in relation to a specific and difficult reciprocal relationship between the person and their environment (Lazarus, 1999). This transactional definition of stress appears complex, but the main point is that it is the way the individual views or perceives the demand that is important. While everyone might see certain demands or stresses as problematic (for example, the challenging behaviour of service users), some people might have much greater tolerance than others. Other demands or stresses may have little or no effect on some people, while other people might be sensitive to their effects. The circumstance in which an individual experiences demands or stresses is also going to play an important part. For example, stresses and demands may be ameliorated by certain characteristics of the environment. That is, challenging behaviour may have little or no effect on staff if they are provided with the appropriate support from colleagues, management or within the environment. All of these factors need to be investigated.

Effects of stress

People often experience unpleasant emotional strain from work but this must be counterbalanced by the fact that a significant number of people do get pleasure from their work, and that a rather greater percentage report pleasure derived from their work on any given day. This suggests that, with careful management, people can enjoy happy and rewarding working lives. In small amounts, stress can be a very useful aspect of the work environment, and it has often been shown that where the levels of stress increase from a low base, this can improve work performance and the quality of work. However, this relationship begins to fail once the level of stress exceeds the person's resources or the support to manage the levels of stress. Once the individual loses the ability to cope, this will have a marked and dramatic impact on work performance, which will deteriorate rapidly as stress increases. If this imbalance between the staff perception of demands on them and their coping resources is prolonged, it may lead to burnout. This has a number of significant implications for staff well being.

A central feature of burnout is a feeling of a lack of emotional resources, such as tiredness, irritability and low mood. This is accompanied by feelings of depersonalisation (the development in the member of staff of negative attitudes, with a loss of concern, positive feelings, sympathy or respect for the service users they are working with, and feelings of physical exhaustion).

Finally, burnout syndrome is accompanied by feelings of lack of personal accomplishment, which equates with a lack of job satisfaction (Maslach, Jackson & Leiter, 1996). Burnout has been well documented in many types of helping professions, and staff working in human services are particularly susceptible to such situations occurring. Consequently, this is particularly relevent to staff groups who work in learning disability services.

Stress management interventions

It is clear that the impact of stress on staff cannot and should not be ignored. Therefore, what we do about stress is a key issue, because reducing the impact of stress will improve the psychological and physical health of the staff, and improve their performance. This, in turn, will indirectly contribute to the reduction of absenteeism and turnover.

The basis for any intervention would be designed to enable staff working in the organisation to manage the stresses that occur in the work place by:

- identifying individual and staff group stressors
- identifying and prioritising the principal environmental stressors
- identifying sources of support and resources that can be used to counteract the negative effects of stress
- devising collaborative strategies to manage stressors at both the individual and organisational levels.

As such, this emphasises that, although individual members of staff should be enabled to maximise their personal coping resources, for any stress management programme to be effective in the longer term, this has to be supported by the organisation in which they work. This places responsibility on the organisation to provide a working context that supports these changes.

Many interventions are effectively designed as self-contained, one-off packages. Where very difficult problems exist within an organisation (such as staff experiencing high levels of distress), more intensive packages may be necessary. For stress management programmes to be effective in these cases, a number of key elements need to be put into place:

- a focus on stress rather than other associated factors
- the training occurs during and in the context of more general stress reduction efforts
- it is repeated within a regular programme cycle
- it is based on a clear model of stress so that it can be evaluated and improved
- it will be embedded within a problem-solving approach and therefore part of other support groups and projects of organisational change within the working environment.

Conforming to a process of continuous monitoring and review will ensure that interventions are tailor-made to the organisation and, by so doing, their effectiveness will be maximised. The authors have effectively implemented such a programme in a number of community homes, using the 'demands, supports and constraints' model (Firth-Cozens & Payne, 1999) to guide the assessment and intervention process. **Table 9.1** details a summary of the structure of the stress management programme.

Table 9.1: Intervention summary

Initial assessment	Intervention	Progress meeting	Post-intervention summary	Review meeting	Follow up
Two weeks prior to intervention	*One-day workshop*	*Six weeks later (two hours)*	*Five weeks after progress meeting*	*Half-day session*	*A rolling programme*
Questionnaire survey	Basic concept of stress Personal stress management Discussion of assessment results Comparison of results with management perception of issues Problem solving Goal setting	Review progress towards goals Change goals and strategies as necessary	Questionnaire survey	Discussion of second questionnaire Review progress towards goals Change goals and strategies as necessary	Review progress towards goals Change goals and strategies as necessary External facilitator if necessary

During the assessment, staff are asked to rate their perceptions of strain, demands, supports and constraints using the demands and supports questionnaire (Rose, 1999) and the staff support questionnaire (Harris & Rose, 2002). They are also asked to indicate their perceptions of the team they work in using the team climate inventory (Anderson & West, 1999). Assessment within an organisational context (Rose, 1997) enables a clarification of what staff consider to be the most significant influences on their levels of stress, and reports are then provided based on this information.

From the assessment, it is possible to compile a report to discuss with staff and management in a one-day workshop. Within this day, stress models are discussed, the most important influences on perceived stresses are examined and stress management techniques are introduced, along with problem solving techniques, and finally a list of goals are set. These goals are based on addressing the necessary steps that, if followed through, will reduce levels of stress. Examples of goals have included improving the exchange of information between management and staff, implementing regular and structured staff meetings and reviews of internal procedures and structures. This necessitates the identification of individuals to ensure action takes place.

Approximately six weeks after the workshop, a brief review takes place. This enables progress to be monitored and, if appropriate, goals to be updated. Post intervention questionnaires are then administered and the results discussed in a review meeting. Goals are again reviewed and changed as necessary. Regular follow-up meetings are then arranged as part of a process of continual monitoring and review, to ensure the development of tailor-made interventions to enable maximum efficacy. Where it is identified that there are individuals within the staff teams who are experiencing such high levels of stress that it may be considered to indicate a mental health problem, external facilitators experienced in delivering interventions to people experiencing distress could support the stress management process, particularly as recent research has suggested that the additional implementation of cognitive therapy techniques may be effective in reducing stress (eg van der Klink *et al*, 2003).

The results from the use of this approach in our own practice have been favourable, and such clinical work suggests that using a staff-group focus within a problem-solving approach can lead to a significant improvement in the well being of staff and, in turn, an improvement in the quality of care provision.

Conclusion

Research has shown that staff working in services for people with learning disabilities can experience high levels of stress. This can have a significant impact on the well being of staff, and this has serious implications for the delivery of effective services, both in terms of cost due to absenteeism and sickness, and in terms of the quality of care provided. It is clear that improving the well being of the staff pays dividends in enhancing work performance, and therefore, the quality of the service delivery. Consequently, the high levels of stress that staff in learning disability services experience should be considered a high priority for service managers and the professionals who offer staff support. Evidence suggests that stress management programmes can be beneficial in achieving these aims. However, to be effective, it is important that these programmes are developed with the specific needs of the targeted staff group. Evidence suggests that the programme should focus on individual and organisational factors and use a problem-solving approach within the context of ongoing monitoring and review.

References and further reading

Anderson N & West M (1999) *The Team Climate Inventory-Revised*. Windsor: NFER–Nelson.

Firth-Cozens J & Payne R (Eds.) (1999) *Stress in Health Professionals*. Chichester: John Wiley & Sons.

Harris P & Rose J (2002) Measuring Staff Support in Services for People with Learning Disability: The Staff Support and Satisfaction Questionnaire, Version 2. *Journal of Intellectual Disability Research* **46** (2) 151–157.

Hatton C, Emerson E, Rivers M, Mason H, Mason L, Swarbrick R, Kiernan C, Reeves D & Alborz A (1999) Factors associated with staff stress and work satisfaction in services for people with intellectual disabilities. *Journal of Intellectual Disability Research* **43** (4) 253–267.

Hatton C, Rose J & Rose D (2004) Researching staff. In: E Emerson, C Hatton, T Parmenter and T Thompson (Eds) *The International Handbook of Applied Research in Intellectual Disabilities*. West Sussex: Wiley.

Lazarus RS (1999) *Stress and Emotion: A New Synthesis*. London: Free Association Books.

Maslach C, Jackson SE & Leiter MP (1996) *Maslach Burnout Inventory Manual Third Edition*. Palo Alto, CA: Consulting Psychologists Press.

Rose D, Horne S, Rose J & Hastings R (2004) Negative emotional reactions to challenging behaviour and staff burnout. *Journal of Applied Research in Intellectual Disabilities* 17, 219–223.

Rose J (1997) Stress and Stress Management Training. *Tizard Learning Disability Review* **2** (1) 8–15.

Rose J (1999) Demands, Supports and Residential Staff: A Factor Analytic Study. *Journal of Intellectual Disability Research* 43, 268–278.

Rose J, Jones F & Fletcher B (1998) Stress Management: The Impact of an Organisational Intervention on Staff Well-being and Performance at Work. *Work and Stress* **12** (2) 112–124.

van der Klink JJ, Blonk R, Schene AH & van Dijk FJ (2003) Reducing long term sickness absence by an activating intervention in adjustment disorders: a cluster randomised controlled design. *Occupational and Environmental Medicine* 60, 429–437.

CHAPTER **TEN**

Legal and ethical issues I:
Mental Health Act and consent

JANE BARNES, THERESA JOYCE AND STEVE HARDY

Introduction

In this chapter, we will look at the use, or lack of use, of the *Mental Health Act 1983* in relation to people with learning disabilities. We will consider how it can (and perhaps should) be used for the benefit of this group. We will also look at issues of capacity and consent, particularly in relation to those who have mental health problems as well as learning disabilities.

This chapter refers to current law in England and Wales. Scotland has separate legislation for mental health and consent:

> ***The Mental Health (Care and Treatment) (Scotland) Act***
>
> (Scottish Executive, 2003)
>
> Further information and resources can be obtained from the Mental Welfare Commission for Scotland (www.mwcscot.org.uk) and the Mental Health Law Team (Scotland) (www.scotland.gov.uk/health/mentalhealthlaw)

Adults with Incapacity (Scotland) Act

(Scottish Executive, 2000)

Further information and resources can be found at
www.scotland.gov.uk/Topics/Justice/Civil/16360/4927

The use of the *Mental Health Act* (MHA)

The *Mental Health Act* (MHA) is rarely considered when the needs of people
with learning disabilities and psychiatric disorders are assessed. There may be a
number of reasons for this:

- it is not felt appropriate to use the MHA for people with learning disabilities
- consultant psychiatrists and approved social workers may have little experience
  of people with learning disabilities
- practitioners in learning disability teams may not have a good knowledge of
  the MHA
- there is little joint working
- there is a shortage of specialist units
- learning disability consultant psychiatrists do not have access to beds
- acute units are felt to be inappropriate for people with learning disabilities and
  psychiatric disorders
- people with learning disabilities are viewed as 'untreatable'.

We must, however, consider the implications of this situation:

- service users can be left in unsafe situations at home or in placements, which
  may pose a risk to themselves or others
- parents or carers can be left to manage unsafe situations
- mental illness which may be present does not get identified or treated
- autistic spectrum disorders are frequently missed or misdiagnosed
- service users are admitted to hospital informally, without any understanding
  of their rights and without an independent review of their treatment.

How should we be using the *Mental Health Act*?

The MHA is not just about mental illness. It is concerned with the reception, care and treatment of mentally disordered patients. In the MHA, mental disorder means:

> *'mental illness, arrested or incomplete development of mind, psychopathic disorder and any other disorder or disability of mind'.*

Under section 2 of the MHA, a person can be detained in hospital for assessment if it can be shown that:

a) *'he is suffering from mental disorder of a nature or degree which warrants his detention in hospital for assessment (or for assessment followed by treatment) for at least a limited period; and*

b) *he ought to be so detained in the interests of his own health or safety or with a view to the protection of other persons.'*

Under section 3 of the MHA a person can be detained in hospital for treatment if it can be shown that:

a) *'he is suffering from mental illness, severe mental impairment, psychopathic disorder or mental impairment and his mental disorder is of a nature or degree which makes it appropriate for him to receive medical treatment in hospital; and*

b) *in the case of psychopathic disorder or mental impairment, such treatment is likely to alleviate or prevent a deterioration of his condition; and*

c) *it is necessary for the health or safety of the patient or for the protection of other persons that he should receive such treatment and it cannot be provided unless he is detained under this section.'*

You will note that there are four classifications of mental disorder and that the term 'treatment' (not 'cure') is used. The memorandum to the MHA states that the treatability test will be satisfied if treatment 'is likely to enable the patient to cope more satisfactorily with his disorder or its symptoms, or it stops his condition from getting worse'.

We should also look at what the MHA means by treatment, because it does not just include medication. For the purposes of the MHA, medical treatment includes nursing care, habilitation and rehabilitation under medical supervision.

You will note also that the criteria do not just talk about the person's health, but also his or her safety and the safety of others.

What is mental impairment?

In the MHA, 'mental impairment' means:

'a state of arrested or incomplete development of mind (not amounting to severe mental impairment) which includes significant impairment of intelligence and social functioning and is associated with abnormally aggressive or seriously irresponsible conduct on the part of the person concerned'.

'Severe mental impairment' means:

'a state of arrested or incomplete development of mind which includes severe impairment of intelligence and social functioning and is associated with abnormally aggressive or seriously irresponsible conduct on the part of the person concerned'.

How do we know whether someone fulfils the criteria for mental impairment?

It is important to obtain information from all sources and, if possible, carry out a joint assessment using professionals from both learning disability and mental health services. Chapter 30 of the *Code of Practice to the Mental Health Act* (Department of Health and Welsh Office, 1999) provides guidance on a number of issues of particular importance to this group of people. It may also be helpful in facilitating communication between teams. In recent years the criteria for receiving a service from specialist teams have been drawn tighter and tighter, and users can fall through the gaps.

It is worth pointing out that the criteria say nothing about IQ. Although services are often based on whether a person has an IQ under 70, the MHA makes no such distinction. The *Code of Practice* (MHA, 1999) says the judgement as to the presence of severe or significant impairment of intelligence 'must be made on the basis of reliable and careful assessment'. Psychological testing may not have been undertaken, but there may be evidence of special schooling or a statement of educational needs in the past.

The *Code of Practice* (MHA, 1999) goes on to say that the evidence for severe or significant impairment of social functioning 'should be based on reliable and recent observations, preferably from a number of sources such as social workers, nurses and psychologists'. We would suggest that this should also include carers and day care workers – in fact, anybody who has regular contact with the person. Evidence may be provided by an inability to self-care, maintain employment or keep safe from exploitation by others.

The *Code of Practice* (MHA, 1999) advises that an assessment of abnormally aggressive behaviour should be based on observations of behaviour which causes 'actual damage and/or real distress occurring recently or persistently or with excessive severity'. An assessment of irresponsible conduct should also be based on observations of behaviour 'which shows a lack of responsibility, a disregard of the consequences of action taken and where the results cause actual damage or real distress, either recently or persistently or with excessive severity'.

So why is the MHA not used?

Even when a person with learning disabilities fulfils the criteria under mental illness, mental impairment, severe mental impairment or psychopathic disorder, the MHA may still not be considered. Many practitioners hold the view that it is not appropriate to use the MHA for people with learning disabilities. This assumes that the MHA is, by definition, oppressive and ignores the fact that users' rights may be better protected. Historically, people with learning disabilities have been placed in institutional care for long periods of time without any system of independent review. Community care is now a reality for most but, if they require treatment for psychiatric disorders in hospital, should this always be on an informal basis (ie without the use of the MHA)? If they do not realise that they can leave or refuse treatment, if their experience of life is always doing what they are told, and if they do not have access to independent review by managers' hearings or mental health review tribunals, then where is the protection of their rights?

It is frequently stated that an acute unit is not an appropriate place for a person with learning disabilities and psychiatric disorders to be treated and therefore admission, whether under the MHA or not, is not considered. There may be concerns about vulnerability which are well founded, but leaving the person where he or she is may put them at even greater risk.

Guardianship

Guardianship under section 7 of the MHA was intended to be of use to this group, and it talks about guardianship being 'necessary in the interests of the welfare of the patient or for the protection of other persons'. The number of guardianship applications has decreased dramatically since 1983, probably because the criteria for mental impairment (which include abnormally aggressive or seriously irresponsible conduct) still have to be met. Those areas of the country that do use guardianship tend to have an approved social worker who believes it is useful, and who uses the MHA creatively.

'It provides an authoritative framework for working with a patient, with a minimum of constraint, to achieve as independent a life as possible within the community.'

Code of Practice to the Mental Health Act (Department of Health and Welsh Office, 1999)

A comprehensive care plan is required, which includes arrangements for suitable accommodation, access to activities and education, treatment and personal support. The guardian can be a named person or the local authority, but the application must be accepted by the local authority in any event.

As well as placing certain requirements on the person, including the requirement to live in a specified place, guardianship provides support for carers and ensures that services stay involved, because they have a monitoring and reviewing role. People with learning disabilities are often left in situations which are infrequently reviewed, and carers are left to manage difficulties with inadequate support.

How is an assessment under the MHA organised?

In order for someone to be detained in hospital under section 2 or 3 or made subject to guardianship, there must be two medical recommendations and an application by an approved social worker (ASW) or the nearest relative (in practice, applications by nearest relatives are rare). One of the medical recommendations must be from a doctor who is registered under section 12 of the MHA. This is usually a psychiatrist. Ideally, one of the doctors should have previous knowledge of the person being assessed, and this is often the GP. The two doctors must have seen the person within five days of each other.

The ASW must be employed by the local social services department and is required to look at all the circumstances of the case, not just the medical issues, and to consult with the nearest relative as well as interview the person concerned. The ASW application must be made within 14 days. If it is not possible to locate the nearest relative, the ASW can go ahead if it is felt that consultation is not reasonably practicable or would involve unreasonable delay. If there is consultation and the nearest relative objects to the making of a section 3 order or guardianship, then the application cannot go ahead without taking the case to court. A section 2 order can go ahead, however, even if the nearest relative is objecting.

If carers or members of the family feel that there should be an assessment under the MHA, they can contact the GP in the first instance, who would then liaise with social services. There is a duty on social services to direct an ASW, as soon as practicable, to take the person's case into consideration, if requested by the nearest relative. An ASW has a responsibility to look at the least restrictive alternative to detention in hospital, so the outcome may be support or treatment in a different setting, provided in the home or on an outpatient basis.

What happens if the person being assessed for a mental disorder lacks the capacity to make a decision?

In paragraph 2.8 the MHA *Code of Practice* (Department of Health and Welsh Office, 1999) says:

> *'If at the time of admission, the patient is mentally incapable of consent, but does not object to entering hospital and receiving care or treatment, admission should be informal.'*

This guidance was issued as a direct result of the House of Lords ruling in the Bournewood case in June 1998.

The Bournewood case

The Bournewood case concerned Mr L, a man with severe learning disabilities who spent 30 years in hospital before moving to live with carers Mr and Mrs E in 1994. Mr L had an autistic spectrum disorder, very little speech, poor life skills and a history of agitated behaviour. Over the following three years he made a gradual improvement, however, to the extent that he required less medication and was attending a day centre.

One day in July 1997, Mr L became agitated at the day centre. Unfortunately, his carers could not be contacted and he was admitted to the learning disability ward at Bournewood Hospital as an informal patient. The consultant did not assess him under the *Mental Health Act* because Mr L neither resisted admission nor attempted to leave the ward. The common law principle was followed, that where a patient does not have the mental capacity to make decisions about medical treatment and the doctor's opinion is that such treatment is in the patient's best interests, then a doctor is entitled to treat without consent.

Mr and Mrs E were asked not to visit Mr L as it was felt that this would distress him and cause a further deterioration in his mental state. After two months, they had still not been able to visit him. They were very unhappy about this and were not convinced that there was any clinical justification for the admission. They also felt it was wrong that Mr L could be returned to institutional care with no greater formality than a consultant psychiatrist's initial assessment. Because Mr L was being treated as an informal patient, there was no right of appeal to an independent review.

Mr and Mrs E consulted a solicitor and a number of legal hearings ensued between October 1997 and June 1998. The Court of Appeal held that consent was essential for informal admission and ordered that Mr L should be assessed under the *Mental Health Act*. This resulted in the making of a section 3, which meant that Mr L now had rights of appeal. An appeal hearing before the hospital managers was held, supported by an independent psychiatric report. The managers ordered Mr L's discharge and he returned home to the care of Mr and Mrs E.

On 25 June 1998, the Bournewood Trust appealed to the House of Lords, and the judgement of the Court of Appeal was overturned. In the view of the Law Lords, therefore, the consultant had not acted unlawfully. However, the effect of this decision clearly troubled Lord Steyn, as it would follow that apparently compliant incapacitated patients would not have the specific protections provided by the 1983 *Mental Health Act*. This has become known as the 'Bournewood gap'.

These protections provided by the 1983 *Mental Health Act* are:

- a formal assessment which involves two medical recommendations and an application by an approved social worker
- rules governing the medical treatments patients are given
- rights of appeal, with legal representation, to an independent legal hearing
- the right to care after leaving hospital.
- the Code of Practice which provides guidance about the interpretation of the MHA and the care of patients
- the Mental Health Act Commission, which has a remit to review the situation of detained patients but not informal patients.

At the time, the Secretary of State assured the House of Lords that reform of the law was under active consideration. So far, we do not have a new MHA. The draft Mental Health Bill has been published and scrutinised by a joint parliamentary committee, which took evidence from concerned parties including the Mental Health Act Commission. The government has published its response (www.dh.gov.uk).

The guidance in the *Code of Practice* raised a number of questions for practitioners involved in these assessments. Firstly, how does someone who lacks capacity object if he/she does not understand what is happening? Why is it that the person who hits out on the way to hospital or verbalises his/her unhappiness gets the protection of the MHA, and the person who can be persuaded does not? Should we be looking for evidence of objection that may not be so obvious (for example, someone who regularly goes to the door of the ward)? Is it not precisely the group of patients who are compliant and least able to advocate for themselves who need the protection of the MHA the most?

The *Human Rights Act 1998*

When the Bournewood case was heard by the House of Lords, the *Human Rights Act* was not an integral part of English law (although it is now). The case was, therefore, taken to Strasbourg and a decision was published on 5 October 2004. The European Court of Human Rights ruled that the circumstances around Mr L's detention amounted to breaches of his rights to liberty and security, and of his right to a review of the legality of his detention.

The implications of this judgement are far reaching and it has been reported that it may result in a review of tens of thousands of people currently being cared for in UK nursing homes and hospitals. Many of these will be people with learning disabilities or dementia who lack the ability to consent to treatment or refuse treatment, and who are being treated on the basis that they are apparently compliant and do not need to be sectioned under the MHA.

The government has conducted a consultation into the way that the Bournewood gap should be addressed in light of the judgement from the European Court for Human Rights, which said that the common law is not robust enough to protect compliant incapacitated adults who need treatment. Considerations include:

• the use of detention under the current MHA

• a modified form of guardianship under the current MHA

• separate protective measures.

How do we assess capacity?

At the moment, we do not have any legislation which tells us how to assess capacity; the new *Mental Capacity Act* passed in 2005 will not come into force until 2007. We do, however, have case law to guide us, and the principles relating to an assessment of capacity are generally accepted. An individual is presumed to have the capacity to make a decision about treatment unless he or she:

- is unable to take in and retain the information material to the decision, especially as to the likely consequences of having or not having the treatment

or

- is unable to believe the information

or

- is unable to weigh the information in the balance as part of the process of arriving at the decision.

The relevant case law here is:

- Re C (refusal of treatment) 1994
- Re MB (caesarean section) 1997

This is a legal concept, not a medical one and is covered by common law, not statute. Where statute law exists (that is, legislation which is laid down by parliament), that will always take precedent. Where somebody is detained under the MHA, therefore, he or she is covered by consent to treatment rules under Part IV of the Act, which authorise treatment for mental disorder. Treatments given for physical disorders and treatment given for mental disorders to patients not covered by Part IV of the MHA are governed by common law. Under common law, a person with capacity can refuse treatment even if that decision is irrational.

To be valid, consent must be freely given, and informed about the effects, risks and alternatives of doing or not doing something. Consent which is given as the result of pressure from someone else is not deemed to be valid. This can be tricky to clarify if a person with learning disabilities has spent his entire life being told what to do by other people. If an adult does not have the capacity to make a decision about treatment, it is the duty of the doctors to exercise their clinical judgement and treat him or her in his or her best interests under the common law doctrine of necessity. *Contrary to popular opinion it is not the responsibility of carers or relatives to make these decisions, although they should be consulted whenever possible.*

Best interests

The definition of best interests was laid down in the case of re:F (mental patient: sterilisation) 1989 and states that:

'Treatment is necessary to save life or prevent a deterioration or ensure an improvement in the patient's physical or mental health; and is in accordance with a practice accepted at the time by a responsible body of medical opinion skilled in the particular form of treatment in question.'

However, if there is doubt about someone's capacity to give consent or the proposed treatment is very significant, the case should be referred for legal advice, as it may need to be taken to court for a decision.

Mental Capacity Act (2005)

Because these issues have been of great concern to practitioners for a long time, the government asked the Law Commission to develop recommendations. These recommendations were published in 1995 and formed the basis for the green paper *Who Decides* in 1997. In 1999, the White Paper *Making Decisions* was published. In 2005 the *Mental Capacity Act* was passed and it is expected to come into force in April 2007.

Definition

The *Mental Capacity Act* states that:

'A person lacks capacity in relation to a matter if, at the material time, he is unable to make a decision for himself in relation to the matter because of an impairment of or a disturbance in the functioning of the mind or brain. It does not matter whether the impairment or disturbance is permanent or temporary.'

Principles in the Mental Capacity Act

- A person must be assumed to have capacity unless it is established that he lacks capacity.

- A person must not be treated as unable to make a decision unless all practicable steps have been taken to help him do so.

- A person must not be treated as unable to make a decision merely because he makes an unwise decision.

- Advises that a decision about someone's capacity must be decided on the balance of probabilities.

- A person is unable to make a decision for himself if he is unable to understand the information relevant to the decision, retain that information, use or weigh that information as part of the process of making the decision or communicate his decision (in any way).

- The fact that a person may only be able to retain the information relevant to the decision for a short period does not prevent him from being regarded as able to make the decision.

- An act done, or a decision made, for or on behalf of a person who lacks capacity must be done, or made, in his best interests.

Conclusion

When assessing the needs of people with learning disabilities, it is the responsibility of us all to know what options are available to us and to use effectively the tools we have. We should not dismiss the current *Mental Health Act* (MHA) as being inappropriate for people with learning disabilities and psychiatric disorders without proper consideration. The MHA might actually be very helpful in ensuring that someone obtains the assessment, treatment and protection he or she requires, as well as supporting the carers who may be so overwhelmed that they cannot make those decisions.

The new MHA may still be some way off, but the Bournewood ruling is very significant. The *Mental Capacity Act* should enable everyone in the future to be clearer about how decisions should be made. In the meanwhile, we have guidance and case law to help us. Abuse of people with learning disabilities can happen in a variety of ways. If we are too paternalistic, we are in danger of taking all decision-making away from them and denying them the opportunity to make those choices of which they are capable. If we leave them to make decisions of which they are not capable, this will put them and others at risk.

Further information

For further information on the *Mental Capacity Act* Implementation Programme, visit www.dca.gov.uk

References and further reading

Department for Constitutional Affairs (2005) *The Mental Capacity Act.* London: HMSO.

Department of Health and Welsh Office. (1999) *Mental Health Act 1983: Code of Practice.* London: HMSO.

HL v United Kingdom 2004 (Bournewood).

Jones R (2004) *Mental Health Act Manual.* 8th edition. London: Sweet and Maxwell.

Lord Chancellor's Department (1999) *Making Decisions. The Government's proposals for making decisions on behalf of mentally incapacitated adults.* London: HMSO.

Lord Chancellor's Department (1997) *Who Decides? Making decisions on behalf of mentally incapacitated adults.* London: HMSO.

Re C (refusal of treatment) 1994.

Re F (mental patient: sterilisation) 1989.

Re MB (caesarean section) 1997.

R v Bournewood Community and Mental Health NHS Trust, ex parte (1998).

Scottish Executive (2003) *The Mental Health (Care and Treatment) (Scotland) Act.* Edinburgh: Scottish Executive

Scottish Executive (2000) *Adults with Incapacity (Scotland) Act.* Edinburgh: Scottish Executive.

CHAPTER ELEVEN

Legal and ethical issues II: Risk assessment and management, and the Care Programme Approach

THERESA JOYCE AND STEPHEN HIGGINS

Definition of risk and risk assessment

There are different definitions of risk, but they all contain the idea that an unfavourable outcome could occur if a particular action is undertaken. The element of risk is the extent to which the unfavourable outcome might occur. If it is certain that something will occur, then there is no risk. The purpose of risk assessment is to attempt to predict the likelihood of a given outcome occurring, given a particular set of circumstances. It is not easy to do this, and a structured approach to the assessment of risk has therefore been developed (Carson, 1991). This approach involves considering 'consequences' and 'likelihood'. This chapter will consider the approach in relation to people with learning disabilities who have additional mental health problems, although the framework can be applied generally.

Risk-taking

The overwhelming message from previous sections and chapters should be that people with learning disabilities are people first. Even where mental health issues exist, principles of the person's rights as a citizen should be balanced with protection principles for the individual. This requires an awareness that people with mental health problems or challenging behaviour present risks to themselves or others. Risk-taking decisions must be considered by a systematic procedure that weighs up the relative benefits, costs and safeguards required in potentially risky situations.

Likelihood

It is important not to deny a person a chance, without considering how dangerous it might actually be for that person. It is best to test out the situation in carefully controlled conditions where possible negative consequences can be minimised. Safeguards should be built in to meet the objective by the least risky means.

Consequences

The consequences of taking the risk also need to be considered. The consequences may be more or less serious for the person themselves or for others, but all should be defined.

Objective

Where an element of risk is involved in an activity, it must be decided whether the objective is an important addition to the enhancement of the person's independence, freedom and quality of life. The benefits to the individual of learning to use public transport could well seem more important than the possible cost, whereas a decision to take part in bungee-jumping or rock-climbing might be more risky for a person with mental health problems and learning disabilities than the likely benefits would warrant. Or not.

Duty of care

Staff working with people with learning disabilities are held in law to have a 'duty of care' towards the users of services. The people who use health and social services are entitled to participate in the activities and opportunities available to ordinary citizens, although they may need extra support to enable this to occur. Staff should take reasonable care in all circumstances, but should allow and encourage reasonable risk-taking. The duty of care requires that staff protect service users from harm.

However, this can sometimes become overprotection, which then denies the person choice and access to a full life. People with learning disabilities may also not be able to judge risk for themselves and may need help in learning how to do this. Staff also need to be able to examine the risks that are likely to occur for service users in specific situations, in order to judge a) if the risk should be taken, and b) if it is, what action can be taken to minimise it. This is even more relevant for people with additional mental health problems, as their difficulties may mean that risk also has to be judged in relation to the person's mental state at a particular time.

Risk in community services

People with learning disabilities are now much more likely to be living in ordinary communities than was the case many years ago, when services used to be very institutionally-based. However, there is evidence that people with learning disabilities may be more likely to be victims of crime, bullied or harassed (Mencap, 1999). This risk is likely to be greater than the risk of a person with learning disabilities harming someone else. Public perception of people with mental health problems is that they are more likely to harm than be harmed, but this is not the case. However, it is also important to assess any risk that an individual may present to others.

There is clear recognition that people with learning disabilities also have the right to make choices for themselves (DH, 2001). Risk may also be an element in choice, and it is essential that the person with learning disabilities is involved in any decisions about risk.

Examples of risk that can occur (and which have been reported to the authors):

- risk of assault if inappropriate approaches are made to members of the public when out alone
- risk of bullying or harassment if behaving unusually
- risk of sexual exploitation when out socialising
- risk of financial exploitation from neighbours
- risk of assaulting others when placed in new situations
- risk of getting lost/going missing overnight when travelling independently.

Risk factors

There are a number of factors that need to be considered when assessing the risk in any given situation. These will all contribute to an assessment of the two main dimensions mentioned earlier (ie likelihood of an unfavourable outcome, and the nature of that outcome). For example, the nature of an unfavourable outcome may be that a person will be called names or bullied. The likelihood of that outcome may be high if they go out looking badly dressed, or are agitated. It may be even higher if they then visit a part of the neighbourhood where it is known that this has happened to others, or if they go out at a certain time of day.

In order to make a judgement about risk, good information is needed. Part of that information is based on knowledge of the person and their history, how they usually react in specific situations, how that might be influenced by their mental state at the time, and how they might be influenced by the context of the situation.

Case example

Sam is a 36-year-old woman with mild learning disabilities and a possible diagnosis of bipolar affective disorder. She often behaved in ways that her staff team found very difficult to manage, including throwing things at staff, breaking crockery and furniture, and assaulting staff. She was also extremely interested in children, and was known to approach them and try to talk to them. Their parents found this unacceptable, and would try and remove their children. Sam was therefore no longer allowed to go out alone. Despite being accompanied, however, on two further occasions when parents tried to remove their children, Sam pulled the child's hair. (Both incidents involved girls, and staff related this to Sam being jealous of her sister, who had a daughter.) On one of these occasions the child's father hit Sam and the police were called, but no charges were pursued.

The staff team was becoming anxious about going out with Sam, and said that she should not go out beyond the small complex in which she lived until it had been sorted out.

A risk meeting was called, where the following questions were considered:

1. What was the type of risk being faced by Sam?
2. What was the degree of risk (how likely was it that the risk would occur)?
3. How important was it that the risk is taken?
4. How could the degree of risk be reduced?

5. What would staff do if the risk actually happened?

6. With whom did they need to agree the risk plan?

7. How could they monitor whether the risk plan was working?

The team considered that they needed to gather information on how often Sam had approached children and under what circumstances. Had anything happened before or after that was important? What had staff found to be helpful in trying to make sure that Sam did not approach children? They came up with the following information and plan:

1. The type of risk was that Sam could hurt a child, and that Sam could also be hurt by others. There was also a risk that she could be arrested.

2. The degree of risk was considered to be high, in that, although Sam did not assault a child every time or most times that she went out, she would approach girls aged between six and ten if she saw them. This had occurred in seven out of the previous ten monitored occasions. (This information was gathered from notes taken since staff had started to monitor what happened when Sam went out.)

3. It was also considered to be important to take the risk, as the consequence would otherwise be that Sam would not go out beyond the complex. It would be unacceptable ethically and legally to restrict her in this way.

4. Staff discussed the times Sam had approached girls, the times she had not approached them and the times the children had been assaulted. They identified the following factors:

   i) Sam was most likely to approach children in the local park.

   ii) She was most likely to approach children when the girl was blond.

   iii) It was more difficult to divert her when she was agitated.

   iv) Sam was more likely to be agitated when:

   - she had just had a visit from her mother
   - she did not know which staff were going to be on duty
   - she had had to wait to go out – it had been planned, but then delayed
   - her mental state was worse.

5. Staff agreed that they needed to do a number of things to reduce the risk. The first was, if her mother had visited, to go to places where Sam was less likely to meet children (eg avoid the park). The second was to arrange activities at home if she was very agitated. The third was to go shopping at times of day when children were less likely to be around (eg not at times when children would be

coming home from school). They agreed to make sure that Sam knew in advance who was going to be on shift, and that they would let her know as soon as possible if a shift had to be changed. They also decided to monitor her mental state in a more structured way. A longer-term plan was to arrange individual psychological support to examine her feelings in relation to her family. They would also discuss with her more clearly the possible consequences of assaulting children. Staff also agreed that, if the risk actually occurred (ie Sam did approach a child), they would intervene earlier and try to divert her to another activity. This required staff to be more vigilant when they went out with her. Members of staff would also carry a mobile phone to call for support.

This plan was agreed with the staff team, the service manager, the care manager and specialists from the health team (psychology and community psychiatric nurse). Sam's mother was also involved. Sam did not attend the risk meeting, as she did not want to, so it was discussed with her afterwards. It was agreed to review the plan in six weeks, or earlier if another incident occurred. Monitoring sheets in relation to where Sam went, what her behaviour was like and with whom she went would be filled in on a daily basis.

All those present stated individually that they agreed with the plan.

It is important that assessment is undertaken objectively. If this does not occur, then decisions about risk may end up being taken on the basis of opinion. Psychological evidence suggests that people make decisions in a way that is not necessarily rational or based on evidence, and we need to be aware of this when making decisions on behalf of, or with people with learning disabilities (Eysenck & Keane, 2000).

Part of this objective assessment is to use data and information about the person themselves. This is then used as one of the means of predicting what is likely to occur in the future, but it is essential to recognise that such 'retrospective predictions' are difficult to make accurately. The Department of Health states that 'there have been a number of cases which demonstrate how difficult it can be to make accurate predictions about future risks' and that staff should 'recognise these difficulties and make an honest and thorough assessment based on best possible practice and taking account of all the known circumstances of each case' (NHS Executive, 1994).

Decision-making

If an individual has relatives or an advocate interested in their welfare, it is important to seek their views, but staff should be aware that no-one has a legal right to make a decision on behalf of an adult with learning disabilities. The *Mental Capacity Act* (2005) acknowledges that in some cases, such as small day-to-day decisions, carers can make decisions on behalf of those that lack capacity as long as it is done in their best interests. In this situation, decisions have to be made in the person's best interests (see Chapter 10).

Vulnerability

Assessing risk also involves protecting the service user from abuse. This can include physical, sexual, financial and emotional abuse. There is evidence that people with learning disabilities are more vulnerable to abuse (DH, 2000). Risk assessment procedures may need to be undertaken in relation to reducing the risk of abuse occurring, while ensuring that people's lives are not unduly restricted. Issues of consent are likely to need to be considered in this context (see Chapter 10). Some services users with mental health problems may have been detained in hospital for treatment under the *Mental Health Act*. Discharge will depend, to some extent, on an assessment of the extent to which the person no longer needs treatment for his own health and safety or for the health and safety of others (*Mental Health Act*, DH, 1983). A multidisciplinary team will consider the impact of the mental illness on the behaviour, and treatment of the mental illness is then also a crucial factor in managing risk. For service users in this situation, the Care Programme Approach is then implemented.

Care Programme Approach

The Care Programme Approach (CPA) was developed in the early 1990s as a way to manage care for people who have serious mental health problems, who are living in the community. It was revised in 1999 (DH, 1999) and the new format is currently used within mental health services. People with learning disabilities who have additional mental health problems come under the remit of the CPA process.

The Care Programme Approach and people with learning disabilities

The CPA offers an effective case management process for people who have complex mental health and social support needs. It is a holistic process that acknowledges the whole individual and all those aspects that contribute to a person's mental health, such as finances, daytime activity, daily living skills, housing and physical health. There are a number of potential benefits in supporting people with learning disabilities with mental health problems using the CPA system. These include having a mental health focus, and potentially reducing misdiagnosing signs of mental illness as a normal part of having learning disabilities (Reiss *et al*, 1982). There are also a number of advantages for services of having closer communication and understanding between mental health and learning disability services (Roy 2000; Keys, 1999).

The Care Programme Approach, health action plans and person-centred planning

Valuing People (DH, 2001) recognises that people with learning disabilities are at greater risk of developing a number of physical health problems but are less likely to access primary care services. To reduce inequality and unmet health needs, health action plans are being introduced. A health action plan details the actions needed to maintain and improve the health of an individual, and any help needed to accomplish these (DH, 2002). To reduce duplication in the care of those individuals who have both significant mental and physical health needs, the CPA can also be that individual's health action plan.

In recent years, we have seen a shift in the way in which care is planned and delivered. Services should strive to work in a person-centred way, helping people to work out what they want in life and planning the support they need to achieve their goals and aspirations. Each person with learning disabilities should be offered the opportunity to have a person-centred plan. The CPA process is separate from person-centred planning, but health and social care professionals who are care co-ordinators for an individual who is in receipt of CPA should ensure that they work in a person-centred way.

Components of the Care Programme Approach

There are two levels to the CPA process. The first level, standard CPA, is aimed at supporting people who have mental health problems and are thought to be at low risk of relapsing. They tend to have good family and social support, are likely to stay in touch with services and may only have one or two professionals involved with their care.

The second level of CPA is the enhanced level and this is aimed at supporting people with serious and ongoing mental health problems and who are at risk of relapsing. As with the standard level, these people may be returning home after a period in hospital or receiving mental health care in the community. Other factors that may lead to being placed on the enhanced level are a history of suicide attempts, self-harm, violence, dangerous behaviour and self-neglect. The person may not have good social or family support, may have lots of difficulties in their everyday life, may not maintain contact with services and may need input from several professionals to support them to live at home.

The multidisciplinary team

The CPA is an interdisciplinary process and is an opportunity for the service user, their family and all the professionals involved to get together and plan the person's future care. One professional is allocated as a care co-ordinator (usually the professional who will have most contact with the person).

Care co-ordination

The care co-ordinator should be a health or social care professional who is competent in the delivery of mental health care to people with learning disabilities, and who has knowledge of the service user and a wide range of local services. Their main role is to co-ordinate care by being the main link between the service user, their family, and all involved professionals and agencies. The care co-ordinator should ensure that the care plan is implemented, monitor its effectiveness and promote the service user's involvement in the whole process.

The care co-ordinator is responsible for organising the CPA meetings, making sure everybody involved is invited to the meeting. They support the service user and their family to participate in the meeting, and make sure that everyone receives a copy of the care plan that is agreed at the CPA meeting.

The care plan

Before the care plan is agreed, an assessment of the person's health and social care needs is undertaken by the relevant professionals involved. They submit their reports to the care co-ordinator before the meeting and each area of need is discussed and clarified at the CPA meeting. An important aspect of the CPA care plan is for everyone involved to assess any risks associated with the person.

Once the assessment is agreed, a care plan to meet any needs identified is then discussed and agreed. This will include a risk management plan to reduce the likelihood of the risks occurring, and also how crises should be managed. People are identified who will be responsible for implementing each aspect of the care plan. This helps to ensure that everyone knows what he or she is supposed to be doing to support the service user.

Case example

The following case example highlights the areas of use for CPA and risk management with a person with complex healthcare needs and learning disabilities.

Tom is a 36-year-old man with mild learning disabilities, who lives alone in north London. He moved into his flat after his mother died two years ago. Before this, he had worked in a warehouse for many years and was not known to any services. When his mother died he lost his job and had to leave the family's council flat. In his new flat, he accumulated rent arrears and was taken to court with over £1,500 in arrears. He was eventually referred to the local adult mental health team, because he was saying that everyone was against him and he could hear his mother's voice talking to him. He was prescribed medication to help with this, which he continues to take. Despite this, Tom will often break down in tears and say that he wishes he was dead and he can't go on. He says he has problems with his neighbour, whom Tom claims sometimes shouts at him and who recently asked Tom if he would rent out his flat to a 'friend'.

Tom spends most of his time wandering the streets or sitting in cafes, where he prefers to eat. He did receive a gas cooker from social services but says he is scared it will blow up, as he finds the buttons confusing to use. He has little money and currently receives Job Seeker's Allowance. His social worker (from adult mental health services) states that she thinks he can be lazy and manipulative. She says Tom does not look after himself in order that other people will do it for him, and she cites as an example that she telephoned him to tell him to go and collect his new cooker but he did not turn up on the right day, so it had to be delivered for him. Tom says he has a cousin who lives on the other side of London, who helps him by doing his laundry and giving him cooked food and helping him have a bath and a shave once a week.

Areas for assessment

In trying to manage Tom's case, a number of interrelated difficulties immediately present themselves. These include:

- Tom's mild learning disabilities
- his ongoing emotional and mental health problems
- his financial situation
- his everyday living skills
- his isolation and support network
- accessing appropriate health and social care services
- Tom's occupation.

Tom requires support from a number of agencies to ensure his needs can be met in the short- and longer-term. Typically, he would be placed on enhanced CPA level.

In Tom's case, there are also a number of risk areas that are immediately apparent. These include:

- thoughts of self-harm
- neglect of self-care and inability to meet own self-care needs
- vulnerability.

It is clear that risk management must go hand in hand with the wider care management for Tom, as all these factors are in fact interrelated and need to be addressed simultaneously:

- Tom's idea of wanting to die is related to his mental state, but both are inextricably linked with his financial and social situation, and his feelings of bereavement.

- The risks around self-neglect relate to Tom's current mental state, his everyday living skills and the level of support he has.

- Tom's vulnerability is apparent not only through his learning disabilities, but also through his mental health problems, his lack of good social support and his dependency on others to assist with his financial affairs.

Therefore, while care planning and risk management are often discussed as separate issues, in practice they are different sides of the same coin and both need to be addressed adequately to provide comprehensive support for individuals.

References and further reading

Carson D (1991) Risk taking in mental disorder. In: D Carson (Ed) *Risk taking in mental disorder: analyses, policies and practical strategies*. Chichester: SLE Publications.

Deb S, Thomas M & Bright C (2001) Mental Disorder in Adults who have a Learning Disability. 1: Prevalence of Functional Psychiatric Illness among a 16–64 years old community-based population. *Journal of Intellectual Disability Research* **45** (6) 495–505.

Department of Constitutional Affairs (2005) *Mental Capacity Act*. London: The Stationery Office.

Department of Health (1983) *The Mental Health Act*. London: HMSO.

Department of Health (1999) *Effective Care Coordination in Mental Health Services: Modernising the Care Programme Approach*. London: HMSO.

Department of Health (2000) *No Secrets: Guidance on developing and implementing multi-agency policies and procedures to protect vulnerable adults from abuse*. London: HMSO.

Department of Health (2001) *Valuing People: A New Strategy for Learning Disability for the 21st Century*. London: HMSO.

Department of Health (2002) *Action for Health – Health Action Plans and Health Facilitation*. London: HMSO.

Eysenck M & Keane M (2000) *Cognitive Psychology: A Students Handbook* Fourth Edition. London: The Psychology Press.

Keys R (1999) Care Programme Approach. *Learning Disability Practice* **2** (1) 17–19.

Mencap (1999) *Living in fear*. London: Mencap.

NHS Executive HSG (94)27 (10.05.94) *Guidelines on the Discharge of Mentally Disordered People and their Continuing Care in the Community*. London: HMSO.

Reiss S, Levitan GW & Szyszko J (1982) Emotional Disturbance and Mental Retardation: Diagnostic Overshadowing. *American Journal of Mental Deficiency* 86, 567–574.

Roy A (2000) The Care Programme Approach in Learning Disability Psychiatry. *Advances in Psychiatric Treatment* 6, 380–387.

CHAPTER TWELVE

Autism

PETER CARPENTER AND RICHARD HAMMOND

Introduction

This chapter will look at defining autism and the implications for supporting individuals who fall within the autistic spectrum of disorders.

To enable provision of the right support for an individual with autism, carers need to know and understand the underlying impairments associated with autism, how these individuals experience their environments, and how their environments impact on their behaviour.

Developing an understanding of autism

Autism is a perplexing disorder and our understanding of it has evolved greatly over recent decades, although many questions remain unanswered. We now know much more about the underpinning impairments of autism but continue to search for the exact sites of the brain where the impairments lie and how they operate.

Media attention, through films like Rain Man and television documentaries, has brought autism and its issues to a wider audience. This, however, has not demystified the complexity of the disorder, nor has it dispelled all the myths surrounding autism which are held by the general public.

Many people continue to view those with autism as having special gifts/talents, disliking being touched by others and being prone to temper tantrums. Although these points may be true of some people with autism, they omit the vital understanding of the underlying communication and social impairments of autism.

A historical picture of autism

Autism was first described in the 1940s, when the term was used by two independent pioneers working with children, Leo Kanner (USA) and Hans Asperger (Vienna). Both men used the word to encapsulate some children's inability to relate to others. The children appeared to ignore and disregard what was going on around them, and instead related to objects, occupying themselves for hours playing with items in a repetitive manner. They were rigid in their interests and showed a marked 'desire for sameness'. Some had isolated talents which were quite extraordinary.

The word 'autistic' comes from the Greek word 'autos' meaning 'self'. The word 'autism' was first used by Bleuler, who introduced the term 'schizophrenia' in 1911, and stated that a key characteristic of this was 'autism'. In part due to this shared term, and because schizophrenia was often used to label conditions that were not treatable by psychotherapy, autism was often called 'childhood schizophrenia'.

For many years, there was much debate and disagreement on what caused autism and what autism was. In the 1960s, one psychoanalyst, Bruno Bettleheim, saw the underlying cause of autism to be the inability of the child's 'frozen' parents (particularly the mother) to emotionally bond and interact with their child. Today it is accepted that autism is not a result of emotional deprivation and, thankfully, parents are no longer blamed.

Scientists in many fields continue to look for the causes of autism. Advances in the understanding of the brain's pathology may one day lead us to areas where autism can be 'located' or seen to operate within the brain. Research does indicate that there is likely to be no single cause of autism, but that it may operate in combination with genetic or other factors. Similarly, although certain areas of the brain are likely to be important in the cause of autism, it is unlikely that we will find a single specific area that contains the cause of autism, and we are likely to find that several areas can be affected, to give rise to the impairments of autism.

What is autism?

Autism is defined by changes in behaviour, which demonstrate impairments in three areas of life (known as the 'triad of impairments'):

- impairment in verbal and non-verbal communication
- impairment in two-way social interaction (relationships)
- impairment of imaginative skills and limited interests (rituals and routines).

What constitutes an 'impairment' in any of these areas can be very diverse, and all of these behaviours have a continuum of impairment. Autism itself must be seen as a spectrum, or continuum of disorders. For the characteristics to be considered to constitute a disorder, the person should be distressed or suffering (or causing distress) in all three areas of impairment.

The diagnosis of autism is made by recognising patterns of behaviour from early life. Both the *Diagnostic and Statistical Manual (DSMIV)* (American Psychiatric Association, 1994) and the *International Classification of Diseases (ICD-10)* issued by the World Health Organisation (1993) use the triad of impairments (above) as a basis for diagnosis.

The signs of autism are difficult to detect during infancy, given the limited skills expected of small children, and may go unnoticed by parents (although parents often report that, looking back, they knew something was wrong). As the child gets older, however, the developmental milestone of speech is delayed or not achieved at all, and it is often then that parents begin to question the child's catalogue of odd behaviours and strange lack of interest in others.

Asperger's syndrome

In the 1940s, Asperger's original patients had been more able than those of Kanner and as a result, the term Asperger's syndrome began to be used during the 1980s for those individuals with autism who have average or above average intelligence, in an effort to counter the belief that people had reduced intelligence because they had autism. *DSMIV* and *ICD10* now use the separate category of Asperger's syndrome for people with autism who have almost normal development. However, most people, including clinicians, now use the term Asperger's more widely than *ICD10* or *DSMIV*, to mean anyone with autism who has good speech and is not of low ability.

People with Asperger's syndrome still have impairments in reciprocal social interactions, however, and these often result in a solitary lifestyle (even though the person might feel lonely), language problems and difficulties with non-verbal communication. The all-absorbing, narrow interests of people with Asperger's syndrome make them stand out. They find it difficult to understand that other people have different thoughts and feelings from their own, and this means they automatically impose their routines and interests on others. When they discuss their favourite subjects, their lack of sensitivity to other people's lower capacity for such discussion mean that most encounters are one-sided and tedious. Nevertheless, there are people at the milder end of the spectrum who manage to marry and have successful careers.

The prevalence of autism

Autism occurs across all cultures and all social classes. (This dispels the theories of the 1960s, which saw autism as a middle-class problem.) Autism affects approximately three times as many boys as girls (Wing & Gould, 1979) but in the more able group this rises to six boys for every girl.

Using the narrow, classical 'Kanner' autistic criteria, the prevalence of autism is two to four children in every 10,000 (Fombonne, 1999). This does not appear to have changed substantially over the last 20 years (Wing & Potter, 2002), but during that time there has been greater recognition of the disorder by the public, by teachers and by clinicians. There has also been a recognition that, in the more able, a much greater range of impairments can be included in the triad of impairments. As a result, the frequency of autism with Asperger's has grown to an estimated 60 in 10,000 (and by some estimates as many as 90 in 10,000).

This broadening of the definition of autism and the inclusion of impairments seen in more able people, together with the fact that the term is being recognised by education authorities and attracting resources to children affected by it, the number of children registered as having autism or Asperger's has now grown to 1 (or more) in 200.

Because it is a rare disorder, you would not expect to see more than one child in a family with autism, but this is not the case. Autism appears to run in the family, and 2% of siblings of children with autism are also diagnosed as autistic. There are high rates of abnormal social language among parents of children with autism (Landa *et al*, 1992) and this may highlight the link between autism and inherited genes.

Using the broader definition of autism, approximately 25% of people with autism/ Asperger's also have mild to severe learning disabilities, and 75% have average or above intelligence (Medical Research Council, 2001).

There is a higher rate of occurrence of autism in people with learning disabilities than is found in the general population, and the rate is highest in the more severely disabled. The causes of autism seem to be associated with a higher risk of more general learning disabilities.

The causes of autism

Autism is not an illness, and it is not 'curable'. It is an organic neuro-developmental disorder. The exact causes of autism are not clear, though biological and genetic research into autism is providing more clues as to its origin.

No single medical condition can be seen to be the cause of autism, although links have been made with the following conditions:

- fragile X syndrome
- Rett's syndrome
- phenylketonuria
- tuberous sclerosis
- viral infections (such as congenital rubella)
- difficulties experienced during pregnancy/birth (eg severe prematurity)
- mother over 35 years at time of birth.

However, the links between some of these conditions and autism is still under dispute (see Fombonne, 1999).

There appears to be no single cause of autism; rather, it is thought to be caused by a combination of genetic and biological factors. However, one way of considering the common cause of autism is that neurones within the brain are not communicating well – that they are themselves 'autistic'. Which parts of the brain are affected will determine the phenomenology and associated impairments of the person, but certain skills are affected to achieve an autism diagnosis, namely those skills that lie behind the triad of impairments. These skills seem to be the ones that probably need the highest level of co-ordination and processing within the brain.

The triad of impairments

This section aims to explore in greater detail the difficulties people with autism experience in each of the three areas within the triad of impairments. No two people will present with exactly the same strengths and needs within each of these areas, and individuals may also have more difficulties within one of the triad of impairments than in another, but all people with autism will have some difficulties in each area. They can and do develop skills, however, and may learn strategies to reduce the effects of their difficulties.

Impairment in verbal and non-verbal communication

Communication includes a range of skills. Some people do not communicate using speech or gestures, but indicate their needs by going to get what it is they want (for example, they go to the kitchen if they are hungry). Some may be completely reliant on other people to interpret their needs. Some people with autism communicate by using single words, while others use short phrases or complete sentences. This communication might be to indicate a need, or it might be used as one of a wider range of functions of communication (for example, requesting information). As many as 60% of people with autism develop speech and, of these, 75% will echo speech (Baltaxe & Simmons, 1981).

Communication development

Frequently, the first thing to be investigated in a child with autism is the possibility that they might have a problem with hearing, because where children without autism have an inherent interest in speech over non–speech sounds, children with autism may not focus on speech. It might be the case that, for example, the sound of the refrigerator is of more interest or importance to the child than the sound of people. (Klin, 1991).

Joint attention difficulties are often present (Mundy *et al*, 1990) and the child's attention may be difficult to direct. One of the ways in which language develops is by the carer and child looking at the same item and the carer making comments about the item. This also involves the notion of 'interest sharing', where there is a pleasure in this activity. Children with autism often find other people confusing, however, and may not find the experience of 'focusing attention' interesting, particularly when there are other distractions. If a child's attention is difficult to direct, language learning is at least delayed. It can sometimes mean that the child learns incorrect labels for objects (for example, if they don't look at the object the carer is talking about).

Pointing and understanding gestures are often difficult. The child with autism might not look in the direction of the point, and may instead look at the end of the person's finger. They may not use gestures in the same way as other children and, for example, might not hold out their arms to indicate that they want to be picked up. The child might lead other people to what they want, rather than pointing at it, or they might direct the person to what they want by holding the person's hand and placing it on the object (Frith, 1989).

Children with autism may develop these skills, but at a later stage than other children. This delay will influence the child's learning of language, and difficulties with communication are likely to persist.

Understanding and people with autism

Understanding of words

When their environment contains a number of stimuli, people with autism often have difficulty attending to a single stimulus. For example, they might find it difficult to attend to speech when there are other distractions in the environment. We all find it difficult to listen in very noisy and chaotic environments, but people with autism may be particularly affected by distractions. They might have the need for certain items to be arranged in a particular order, for example, in which case they will find it extremely difficult to understand what someone is saying while they are distracted by the fact that the kettle is not in its 'correct' place.

People with autism might also learn phrases without being able to recognise and separate the constituent words of the phrase into their meanings. They might have learned language as 'chunks' of sounds. In this case, changing the word order may make the sentence meaningless to them.

Gestures and facial expressions can be an additional difficulty for people with autism. Understanding is reliant on a person's knowledge of the intent behind the gesture or expression. If you are not aware of the emotion behind an expression (such as crying), it may just seem to be a strange sound. People with autism may have difficulties in recognising from a person's expression that they are bored, for example. Difficulties in understanding emotion–related words are frequently noted in people with autism. This is partly to do with their difficulties in understanding abstract concepts, but also to do with the difficulties they have with understanding and recognising that people may have thoughts, feelings and beliefs that are different from theirs. (This is to do with the concept of 'theory of mind'.) Tests have shown that when people with autism are asked to give information about what another person thinks or feels, they frequently give information that is consistent with what they would think, given their knowledge and experience, and do not separate this from what others know and experience (Baron–Cohen *et al*, 1985).

Difficulties with understanding will be reflected in the person's own expressive skills. It is usually the case that people understand more than they are able to express, but this is not necessarily the case in people with autism, because they may 'echo' speech. People who use signs may also echo signing. People with autism might use complex sentences but actually understand only some of the words they are using; or their facial expressions might not reflect what they are saying (for example, they might say, 'go away' while smiling).

People with autism may not find the process of communication inherently rewarding. They might have had repeated experiences of unsuccessful attempts to communicate and might be confused about many aspects of the process. This may contribute to people only communicating to make their needs known (for example, to request a drink) but not for the social pleasure that many of us get from engaging in conversation. This will also be reflected in the difficulties people with autism have in learning language and their (frequently) limited vocabularies.

Echoed speech

Echoing may take a number of forms, and can have a variety of communication functions. Echoing can occur in the following combinations (Frith, 1989):

- **immediate–exact** – repeating the same phrase just after another person has spoken
- **immediate–modified** – repeating just after another person has spoken, but changing the phrase in some way; this could be by repeating only part of the phrase, or by missing out part of the sentence or tense markers
- **delayed–exact** – this is an exact repetition which occurs at a later time, a few seconds, a few minutes or longer after it has been heard
- **delayed–modified** – the echoed phrase has been changed in some way and is repeated some time after it has been heard.

Echoing is a normal process in the learning of language. People with autism often continue to echo speech, however, and have great difficulties in using new sentences which are not echoed. They may learn language as 'chunks' without understanding how to break language down into its parts or how to use these parts creatively and flexibly.

Echoing is a skill. It requires an ability to attend selectively to speech, and to the speech of one person. It requires the ability to remember and process the sequences of sounds heard, and to be able to reproduce these sounds in the same order. This can be done without processing the meaning of the words which are being echoed.

Echoing may have a variety of functions, or it may be used without any apparent communicative intent. People might repeat a phrase as a way of taking part in a conversation. It may be used as a request; for example, when asked, 'Do you want a coffee?' the person responds, 'Want coffee'. People usually echo more when they are in stressful situations. Echoing also increases when a person does not understand what other people are saying. Sometimes, familiar words are more likely to be repeated.

Phrases are sometimes learned in association with a particular event. This may or may not be with understanding of what those phrases mean. Being in the same or similar situations to those in which the phrase was first learned may trigger an echo of that phrase.

Recurrent themes can often be observed in an individual's communication. These themes may be around particular interests or around that person's anxieties. They might be phrases that the person uses in situations in which they are confused about what is happening. The person might become 'stuck' in repetitive themes and might persist in these conversations for a long time, once they have started. Strategies to enable people to switch from repetitive themes must be developed.

An understanding of how the individual communicates is essential in the planning of effective support for people with autism. Individuals should be supported to use their existing skills and develop functional communication skills. Speech and language therapists will be able to provide assessment information, plan interventions and support staff to implement these changes to the communication environment.

Social impairments

The impairment of reciprocal social interaction refers to a person's inability to engage in two-way interactions with others and, on a more global level, difficulties forming relationships with others.

Wing and Gould (1979) attempted to measure the degree of social impairment in a group of children with autism, and identified three distinctive groups:

- the aloof
- the passive
- the active but odd.

People in the 'aloof' group appear withdrawn and do not respond to the situations and speech going on around them. They seem to be in a world of their own. They will only seek out others in order to have simple needs met, and this involves leading the carer to the desired object. Eye contact and physical contact with others appears to be avoided, although 'rough and tumble' play or listening to music while being cuddled might be acceptable to some.

People in the 'passive' group accept social approaches with indifference and will often comply with all requests. They could therefore easily be 'led astray'. They have good speech, and will answer questions without hesitation and with complete honesty. They accept social contact as part of life, but it is not something they pursue for pleasure. Difficulties dealing with stresses and changes in routines can cause them great anxiety and will result in emotional displays and/or temper tantrums. They might look shy and anxious, and might have learned to approach adults for instruction.

People in the 'active but odd' group enjoy being with and touching people. They make no distinction between familiar people and total strangers, and lack the understanding of when someone wants contact and when they do not, when it is socially appropriate or socially unacceptable. This causes great difficulties. This group will be known for pestering people and as a result, carers often will not let them out on their own. People in this group can often show, or have a tendency for, physical aggression.

Difficulties using language to communicate

People with autism also have difficulties understanding how other people feel (imagining), or knowing that other people have different thoughts, beliefs or interests. Because of this, they have problems at higher levels of communication:

- difficulties in the use of words to manipulate others (lying, sarcasm, humour)
- difficulties in the boundaries of social interaction (using the right manner of speech for the situation)
- difficulties in regulating social interaction (reciprocal conversation).

Problems with empathy and social interaction

People with autism have problems not only with the communicative aspects of social interaction, but also with their ability to empathise with others – to take an emotional interest in others and share their experiences. Their expectations of friendship are more likely to be those of shared interests, support and spending time together, and not trust, honesty even if it hurts, caring for the other and sacrifice for the other.

Impairment of imaginative skills and limited interests

This impairment highlights the difficulties people with autism face in terms of developing creative and imaginative skills, and in terms of having a narrow area of thoughts and behaviours. As with the other two elements of the triad of impairments, it affects people with autism in different ways and to different degrees, for example, as a repetitive conversational topic (always wanting to talk about bus routes) or as repeated behaviours (spinning a coin or rocking).

Autism is thought to affect the way in which people's brains receive and use information affecting all five senses. Most of the time, we are all faced with huge amounts of information stimulating all our senses, but we filter out what is useful. If this mechanism does not work, the person will quickly become overwhelmed with all the competing information. The incoming information will be jumbled, unclear and confused.

More able people seem to have an inbuilt rule to give most attention to those things that have some meaning or relevance. When we filter new information, we can fit it into what we already know, so that it makes sense even if it is not exactly the same as what we have experienced before. Together, these two methods of 'sorting' new information and updating old information allow us to learn flexibly. People with autism seem to treat and store all information as isolated fragments and are unable to learn flexibly.

This underlying problem explains many difficulties people with autism have in learning and using skills across environments.

People with autism may cope with an environment that they find overwhelming, unpredictable or under-stimulating, by engaging in rigid routines and behaviours to reduce the unpredictability and anxiety they experience. These rigid routines and behaviours may be challenging to those caring for individuals with autism. These routines and rituals can be reassuring and relaxing for the person, however, and we have to find ways of replacing either the routines or the need for them.

Additional difficulties

People with autism show a wide range of additional difficulties that are not necessary for the diagnosis of autism but which seem to be more common in people with autism, and which can markedly impair them.

Physical medical difficulties

People with autism can be medically ill, in pain or in discomfort as much as anyone else, but may not communicate this fact to other people. As with other people with learning disabilities without autism, epilepsy is also more common and may need treatment.

Sensory, processing and motor problems

From observation of people with profound autism and in the accounts of people with Asperger's syndrome, there is wide anecdotal evidence of problems in the senses and motor system. Every sensory modality has been implicated, but those of hearing, sight and touch are the most commonly noted. People can have problems:

- in being over–sensitive
- in being under–sensitive
- filtering information
- modulating input.

These problems can occur across the whole sensory modality or in only part of it (so, for example, the person might have problems with only one level of pitch of sound or one part of the light spectrum). These problems are noted by observation and usually mean the person's physical environment needs to be modified to reduce their stress levels.

There is also a higher incidence of measurable processing difficulties. For example, the person might have problems registering verbal information, or with hand–eye coordination.

It is also recognised that, in people with autism, there is a high number of motor difficulties with features of catatonia and, for example, they can have difficulty initiating actions, or freeze mid–action (Wing & Shah, 2000).

Mental health problems

Relatively little research has been undertaken on the co-morbidity of autistic spectrum disorders and mental health problems, and the majority of these have concentrated on people with Asperger's syndrome (Saulnier & Volkmar, in press). Several studies have suggested that there are increased rates of mental health problems among people with autism who have learning disabilities (Bradley *et al*, 2004; Morgan *et al*, 2003). More recently, a study by Tsakanikos *et al* (in press) found that people with autism and learning disabilities were no more likely to receive a psychiatric diagnosis than those with only learning disabilities.

Attention deficit hyperactivity disorder is a common associate of autism and may need treatment in its own right. Anxiety and obsessional rituals are virtually universal in people with autism, but in many people such rituals reach the level of being disorders in their own right, and needing treatment as such. The anxiety can also crystallise into panic attacks or phobias. With obsessions, the main issue is to determine whether the ritual is driven by anxiety or pleasure. In the latter case, the matter is not an obsession in the psychiatric sense.

All of these conditions may need treatment (environmental treatments and, if needed, medication) to reduce anxiety and enable the person to function.

Mood disorders are very common at the level of both rapid mood swings and mood instability but also, more importantly, at the level of major mood swings in the manner of depression or mania. How these mood swings exhibit themselves is little different to the way they appear in people with learning disabilities. The person may well not have the vocabulary to describe how they are feeling (see Chapter 2).

Paranoia is common in more able people with autism, as it is in people who have some form of isolation from the world (for example, people who are social isolated or deaf). People with autism can hallucinate, and probably do so more often than the rest of the population, but it is easy to misinterpret many of the behaviours of people with autism as being in response to a hallucination.

Support for people with autism

There have been many approaches to treatment and support of people with autism. New ones often appear, while others drift away into obscurity. Approaches to autism arise from the prevailing theories of the nature of autism. With our greater understanding of the underlying triad of impairments, we can be certain that by addressing this triad, we can enable people with autism to participate more fully in our 'non-autistic world'.

When we cannot communicate or interact with others in a meaningful way, we feel and behave differently. There are also differences in our behaviour between when we understand what is happening and when we do not. There are many parallels between our responses in these types of situations and those of people with autism.

The alternative methods of support advocated here stem from the acknowledgement of the three main areas of difficulty experienced by people with autism: verbal and non-verbal communication; social interaction; and restricted activities and interests.

It is likely that a person who has no idea of what is happening will see any demand from others as unpredictable and intrusive. A person with autism may have to resort to focusing on the only aspects of predictability that they have, such as meal times, staff/shift changes and their own repetitive routines/behaviours. The day will probably seem long and stressful for the person with autism, who has no clear idea or understanding of what will happen next. A predictable, structured approach is crucial when supporting people with autism.

Just as we do not like our habits to be prevented, it is important to remember that these things are very important to people with autism and will require negotiation with them. If these routines/rituals are limiting or harming for the development of a person's skills and quality of life, then ways will need to be developed to find rewarding and appropriate alternative behaviours. The long-term aim should not be to eliminate these habits but to reduce them, to allow the person with autism times and places for the habits (in other words, set limits for the person) and to ensure that the person with autism understands this (ie when they can do them).

There are clear ways we can make strange and unpredictable situations more predictable and, as a result, less stressful for people with autism. These 'supports' are practical (for example, visual timetables) and can be developed to make life easier for people with autism, allowing them to know and make choices around their daily lives. Information needs to be present in the environment to inform and remind people of what they will be doing, when they will be doing it and who will support them in the activity. This can be done in a variety of ways to meet the communication needs of the individual (see, for example, Caldwell & Willan, 2003).

When people are this easily distracted, information from language, which is very temporary, can be lost as soon as the speaker stops speaking. Language is often difficult for them to use, even if it can be understood.

In order to reduce the stress of so many distractions, it is important to reduce anything which is irrelevant, when supporting people with autism. The use of very clear language, aided by object/visual cues where appropriate, will prove very effective in increasing the individual's understanding. When carrying out tasks, it can often be useful to follow universal rules such as starting on the left and finishing on the right. Open-ended, creative activities are more difficult than clear tasks with predictable starts and finishes.

By understanding what people with autism are likely to find difficult and the areas where they need support, we can ensure that we provide helpful environments and support which will maximise their potential.

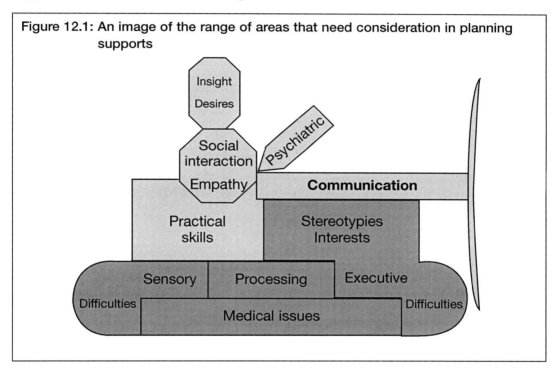

Figure 12.1: An image of the range of areas that need consideration in planning supports

Conclusion

By addressing the underlying triad of impairments, we can enable people with autism to participate more fully in our 'non-autistic world'. Communication is a key factor in people's daily lives. It is vital to recognise an individual's communication strengths and needs, the need for predictability and structure and their difficulties with social interactions. Support should be provided on an individual basis, with environments tailored to meet people's needs. This is necessary to enable individuals to learn and use skills, and to participate in daily living.

References and further reading

American Psychiatric Association (1994) *Diagnostic and Statistical Manual IV.* Arlington: American Psychiatric Publishing Inc.

Baltaxe C & Simmons J (1981) Disorders of language in childhood psychosis. In: J Darby (Ed) *Speech Evaluation Psychiatry.* New York: Grine and Statton.

Baron-Cohen S, Leslie AM & Firth U (1985) Does the child have a theory of mind? *Cognition* 21, 37–46.

Bradley EA, Summers JA, Wood HL & Bryson SE (2004) Comparing rates of psychiatric and behavioural disorders in adolescents with young adults with severe intellectual disability with and without autism. *Journal of Autism and Developmental Disorders* 34, 151–161.

Caldwell P & Willan S (2003) *Can We Talk? Getting in touch with people with severe learning disabilities who have little or no speech – and whose disability is linked to autistic spectrum disorder (ASD): A handbook for families and carers.* Published on www.nwtdt.com (publications section).

Fombonne E (1999) The epidemiology or autism: a review. *Psychological Medicine* 29, 769–86.

Frith U (1989) *Autism, Explaining the Enigma.* Oxford: Basil Blackwell.

Gilberg C, Persson E, Grufman M & Themner U (1986) Psychiatric disorders in mildly and severely mentally retarded urban children and adolescents: Epidemiological aspects. *British Journal of Psychiatry* 149, 68–74.

Klin A (1991) Young autistic children's listening preferences in regard to speech: A possible characterisation of the symptom of social withdrawal. *Journal of Autism and Developmental Disorders* 20,1.

Landa R, Piven J, Wzorek MM, Gayle JO, Chase GA & Folstein SE (1992) Social language use in parents of autistic individuals. *Psychological Medicine* 22, 245–54.

Medical Research Council (2001) *Review of Autism Research: Epidemiology and Causes.* London: Medical Research Council.

Morgan CN, Roy M & Chance P (2003) Psychiatric co-morbidity and medication use in autism: a community survey. *Psychiatric Bulletin* 27, 378–381.

Mundy P, Sigman M & Kasari C (1990) A longitudinal study of joint attention and language development in autistic children. *Journal of Autism and Developmental Disorders* 20, 1.

Saulnier C & Volkmar F (in press) Mental health problems in people with autism and related disorders. In: N Bouras and G Holt (Eds) *Psychiatric and behavioural disorders in developmental disabilities and mental retardation* Second Edition. Cambridge: Cambridge University Press.

Tsakanikos E, Costello H, Holt G & Bouras N (in press) Psychopathology in adults with autism and intellectual disability. *Journal of Autism and Developmental Disabilities.*

Williams D (1993) *Nobody Nowhere.* London: Corgi Books.

Williams D (1994) *Somebody Somewhere.* New York: Doubleday.

Wing L (1981) Asperger's syndrome: a clinical account. *Psychological Medicine* 11, 115–29.

Wing L (1996) *The Autistic Spectrum: A guide for parents and professionals.* London: Constable.

Wing L & Gould J (1979) Severe impairments of social interaction and associated abnormalities in children: Epidemiology and classification. *Journal of Autism and Developmental Disorders* 9, 11–30.

Wing L & Potter D (2002) The epidemiology of autistic spectrum disorders: is the prevalence rising? *Mental Retardation and Developmental Disability Research Reviews* **8** (3) 151–61.

Wing L & Shah A (2000) Catatonia in autistic spectrum disorders. *British Journal of Psychiatry* 176, 357–62.

World Health Organisation (1993) *The International Classification of Diseases (ICD-10) Classification of Mental and Behavioural Disorders: Diagnostic Criteria for Research.* Geneva: World Health Organisation.

Videos

A is for Autism

Directed by Tim Webb. A Finetake Production for Channel 4, 1992. Available for purchase from the BFI (British Film Institute).

This is a short, 11-minute animated documentary film about the experience of autism from the individual with autism's perspective, and offers great insight into their condition.

Learning the Language: building relationships with people with severe learning disability, autistic spectrum disorder and other challenging behaviours. A training video for staff.

Phoebe Caldwell. (Brighton, Pavilion)

A 25-minute video that follows Phoebe attempting to communicate and interact with a profoundly impaired, and challenging man with autism, using techniques drawn from intensive interaction.

CHAPTER THIRTEEN

Mental health problems in older people with learning disabilities

VICKY TURK AND KAREN DODD

Introduction

This chapter looks at the significance of mental health problems that occur when people with learning disabilities grow older, focusing primarily on dementia.

Ageing is a normal stage of the life cycle. In the general population, people are living longer and staying in better health. People with learning disabilities are also living longer, although they still have a significantly lower overall life expectancy. This seems to be due to multiple factors, including:

- people having organic conditions/syndromes/physical and neurological conditions associated with reduced life expectancy

- people in the above groups having increased vulnerability to early onset dementia – particularly true of adults with Down syndrome, and particularly related to Alzheimer's (discussed later)

- people with profound and multiple disabilities having substantially reduced life expectancy

- the fact that, as people live longer, they suffer increasingly from diseases such as cancer and heart/circulatory problems. These conditions may be detected later in adults with learning disabilities and lead to a worse prognosis.

Valuing People (DH, 2001) emphasises that older people with learning disabilities have the same rights to services as older people in the general population. It also recognises that services may need to be provided at an earlier age (for those aged 50 years and above). Planning should be person centred, and particularly sensitive to each person's preferences. *Valuing People* demanded that health issues be addressed through health action plans and health facilitation. If the person has or develops a diagnosed mental health problem, they should be part of the CPA process (see Chapter 11) and have an individualised relapse prevention plan.

It is important to remember that older age does not exclude the needs of people with learning disabilities being addressed through the full range of learning disability and generic policies, procedures and guidelines (eg vulnerable adults, consent to treatment, confidentiality, advocacy, carers assessments).

What are the particular risks associated with ageing for adults with learning disabilities?

Many people with learning disabilities do not have a detailed understanding of the normal life cycle. Often, they are in services for the whole of their lives, services which do not differentiate between the needs of younger and older people. Services need to begin to develop strategies to respond to the growing numbers of older people with learning disabilities, who may require a different style of service.

As with the general population, some health and social changes are more likely to occur for older people.

In health terms, people often become frailer as they age, and their immune systems become less efficient. Hence, diseases can develop more easily and the person may take longer to recover. Existing sensory difficulties (such as hearing and sight problems) often deteriorate, and new sensory problems may develop. Reduced exercise and mobility can increase the risk of falls and bone fractures, cardiovascular disease, skin problems, arthritis and constipation.

Medical interventions need to be sensitive to these factors, particularly the increased risks of toxicity with medication.

In social terms, ageing is a time when there is a greater risk that major life events will happen. These can include the death of parents, spouse, siblings or close friends. Family networks often change, with adult children moving away. People with learning disabilities often have smaller social networks and therefore are more at risk of becoming isolated.

The assessment of an older person with learning disabilities is a lengthy, often complex process. Each person has different cognitive and functional abilities, and different past/current social circumstances. An assessment involves obtaining a detailed history from the person (where possible) and those that know them best, and assessments of health, behaviour and cognitive abilities, together with medical/psychiatric investigations. Depending on the way local services are organised and delivered, the following professionals/organisations are usually involved:

- GP/primary care staff
- specialist hospital services
- community learning disability team (CTPLD) professionals.

The role of GP/primary care staff is to co-ordinate the overall provision of primary healthcare and ensure that existing health problems are diagnosed and treated. They will refer to more specialist services where required, to ensure that all appropriate investigations are completed. Many problems can be effectively treated, giving the older person with learning disabilities an improved quality of life. Particular attention should be paid to issues of pain, foot care, and dental care.

The role of specialist hospital services is to offer specialist investigations for the whole range of conditions that may affect an older person. This includes neurology (where there are concerns about brain function), rheumatology, cardiac and respiratory medicine, and geriatric medicine.

The role of local community learning disability (CTPLD) professionals is that it is often a member of the CTPLD team who is alerted first to concerns about changes in the health, skills, behaviour or life circumstance of the person concerned. Many are now developing clinical pathways to ensure that an efficient assessment occurs, which aids the diagnostic process. Different professionals within CTPLD have different contributions to make to the assessment management plan.

The mental health problems of older people with learning disabilities

Other sections of this reader deal in detail with the presentation and treatment of all the major mental health problems in people with learning disabilities, other than dementia. People can develop the full range of mental health problems in old age, either for the first time or as reoccurrences from earlier in their lives. As with all adults with learning disabilities, if the person is non-verbal it is often very difficult to ascertain the underlying problem(s) and therapeutic interventions may need to be tried to see if they help to alleviate symptoms.

The risk of becoming depressed increases as people with learning disabilities get older, with all the health and social consequences of this. People with depression are typically seen to slow down both physically and mentally, and become withdrawn. Usually their appetite and sleep patterns are adversely affected. Life events are a significant risk factor for the development of depression, and may also mask the early signs of dementia. The symptoms of depression are similar to the early signs of dementia, and in some people depression and dementia occur simultaneously.

The main differences to look for include:

- people with depression are more aware of their problems, and anxious as to their cause

- people with depression have not lost skills/abilities but often are not able to use them because of their mental state

- patterns of night-time disturbance differ, for people with depression more likely to have problems in getting to sleep and waking early, while people with dementia are more likely to get upset in the evenings and have problems with night wandering.

Older people with learning disabilities benefit from the full range of pharmacological and psychological interventions for depression. In instances where the differential diagnosis between depression and dementia is not clear, a brief trial of antidepressants may ease symptoms and/or help to clarify the primary diagnosis.

What is dementia, and is it such a key issue?

Dementia is a general term used to describe a collection of illnesses with a similar pattern of symptoms manifesting in a global deterioration of functioning, leading to a premature death.

Mental Health in Learning Disabilities **A reader** © Pavilion Publishing (Brighton) Ltd 2005

Alzheimer's disease is the most common form of dementia and is a slowly progressive, non-reversible condition characterised by deterioration in cognitive and functional ability, affecting mood, personality and behaviour. It is characterised by changes in the brain consisting of plaques, tangles and neuronal degeneration. The next most common form of dementia is vascular dementia, which is characterised by damage to a number of localised parts of the brain by damaged blood vessels.

Valuing People (DH, 2001) emphasises the special needs of those who develop Alzheimer's disease, saying that 'providing good quality support for these individuals is a major challenge'. The issues are more pertinent due to a number of factors, including:

- increased life expectancy of people with learning disabilities, particularly people with Down syndrome
- the growing awareness of the issues in learning disabilities services
- the increasing number of people being diagnosed with dementia.

The major risk factors for the development of dementia in people with learning disabilities are having Down syndrome, followed by having had a head injury. The incidence of dementia in people with learning disabilities without genetic or neurological cause is thought to be about 5% for those over the age of 65, which is similar to that in the general population. However, the incidence for people with Down syndrome is much greater. Prasher (1995) found age-specific prevalence rates of 9.4% at age 40–49, 36.1% at age 50–59, and 54.5% at age 60–69. The average age of onset was 54, and the average duration from diagnosis of dementia to death was 4.6 years.

Characteristics of Alzheimer's disease in people with Down syndrome

A three-stage model is often used to describe the clinical progress of the disease, with the stages occurring over different time periods in different individuals. Some symptoms may be expressed differently, and not all the signs may be observed in all people.

The main signs seen at each stage are:

Early stage

- Subtle changes in behaviour and mood

- Performance at day placements deteriorates

- Problems with memory, particularly for recent events

- Ability to learn new information is affected

- Language and word-finding problems

- Decline in social, community and daily living skills

- Disorientation

- Difficulties with steps, stairs and kerbs due to depth perception problems

Middle stage

- Memory losses become more pronounced and the individual may forget personal information or the names of familiar people

- Language problems become more evident – the person might have trouble in maintaining a logical conversation, understanding instructions or naming familiar objects

- Confusion and disorientation about time and place, and problems finding their way around familiar environments

- Difficulties with, and then loss of, self-care skills

- More severe changes in personality and social behaviour (eg mood changes, inactivity or apathy, behavioural disturbances such as wandering, sleep problems, agitation, hallucinations and delusions)

- Physical problems, including the onset of seizures, decreased mobility and incontinence

Late stage

- Loss of eating/drinking skills

- Problems with walking and balance; individuals become chair/bed-bound

- Problems with recognising people

- Increase in stereotyped behaviour

- Often require 24–hour care
- Can become bedridden and inactive
- Greater risk of infections, particularly pneumonia

For adults with severe and profound disabilities, symptoms appear to be primarily social withdrawal, apathy and impaired attention. Many of the early signs of dementia can be due to a range of other treatable conditions. These include depression, thyroid problems, sensory difficulties, other physical, psychological and psychiatric problems and environmental changes. It is vital that these are considered as part of the assessment process, and that suitable interventions are put into place as appropriate.

A diagnosis of dementia can only be made once all other possibilities have been excluded, and where the person's level of functioning is known to have declined in comparison to how they functioned at a previous time. Best practice now recommends that baseline assessments of all adults with Down syndrome should be carried out at about the age of 30 (Dodd *et al*, 2003). These should include assessments of cognitive functioning and adaptive living skills, and should be carried out in both residential and day settings to give a detailed picture of how the service user is functioning.

Reliable diagnosis can only occur when the following assessments have been completed:

1. Background history (eg medication, medical history, health status, past abilities, risk factors such as head injury, family history of Alzheimer's)

2. Medical assessment (eg hearing, sight, blood tests, CAT/MRI scans)

3. Psychosocial/psychiatric assessment (eg mental health problems, recent life events, bereavement, social and physical environment)

4. Cognitive assessment (eg orientation, memory, learning, language, visuospatial skills

5. Adaptive assessment (eg daily living skills, social and communication skills)

6. Behavioural assessment (eg changes in behaviour, personality, unusual or challenging behaviours).

What is the value of early diagnosis?

The use of new drug treatments with people with learning disabilities are in their infancy, but there is evidence from a double blind, placebo–controlled pilot study and a further follow-up study, that donepezil hydrochloride (Aricept) shows some efficacy in the treatment of symptoms of mild to moderate Alzheimer's disease in adults with Down syndrome (Prasher *et al* 2003, Prasher *et al*, 2002). Early detection also ensures that management strategies are put in place to help maintain independence and quality of life. Early detection provides information on the current and future numbers of people with Down syndrome developing dementia. This is vital for the person, their carers, service providers and commissioners in order to plan appropriate services and ensure necessary resources are in place.

Who do you tell and when?

Sharing concerns about the possible onset of dementia with affected individuals is an ethical dilemma for which there are not, as yet, clear guidelines. Best practice recommends that baseline assessments should be carried out with all adults with Down syndrome at the age of 30, but what do we tell the person with Down syndrome about why we want to do these assessments? Many people can understand if we explain carefully and in simple terms. However, is it ethical to leave out the fact that we are doing this because of the higher risk of developing dementia, although we don't know whether it will happen to them? Is it justified to say that we are merely collecting information for the future? What will be the effect on the person and their family if we raise their anxieties that dementia is a possibility? Are we being overprotective if we say nothing?

Management of people with dementia

Good care management is central to the care of people with learning disabilities with dementia. Care managers need to have knowledge of the main issues in relation to dementia, in order to ensure that services are co-ordinated without unnecessary delays or duplication. Cases should not be closed once a diagnosis of dementia has been confirmed. Good care management will ensure improved planning and liaison between specialist learning disability services, primary health care services, social services, secondary health care services and the private and voluntary sector, in order to meet the needs of the person.

The person's needs have to be reviewed regularly. Risks also need regular reassessment and monitoring (for example, every three months). Care managers need to plan ahead, anticipating the person's needs at the next stage of the dementia and identifying possible solutions.

The person with dementia should be cared for within their familiar environment if both the environment and the care offered can meet their changing needs. In many instances, this can be achieved through a combination of environmental adaptations and an increase in the level of support provided to staff or family carers. In residential settings, this may necessitate liaison and negotiation with the local inspectors from the National Care Standards Commission to ensure that registration requirements can be met. Outreach support staff who can work with existing carers in their own homes, can also help to maintain the person in their home environment.

In some situations, a move is needed, particularly if the environment is unsuitable and cannot be adapted, the level of care is not available or family carers can no longer cope. This decision is particularly difficult to make if the person with dementia is living with an elderly carer and they have been (or are) mutually dependant.

If a move is needed, it is important to try to find a new home where the person can live the remainder of their life without further moves.

Appropriate environments can help to minimise the effects of the dementia. Ground floor facilities are required, to cater for people in wheelchairs. Simple adaptations can help, for example, painting toilet doors red can improve orientation and help to keep the person continent, because it makes it easier for the person to identify where the toilet is. Good practice in environments can be found in *Down's syndrome and dementia, A Practitioner's Guide* (Kerr, 1997).

Caring for the person with dementia requires carers to have a flexible approach, keeping the needs of the person at the centre. Making the routine suit the person, rather than trying to fit the person into a tight routine, is often the key to success. In the early stages of dementia, the emphasis is on maintaining skills by increasing staff supervision and prompting. Using memory aids such as diaries and timetables can help, as can keeping verbal requests simple and clear, and using additional cues and prompts. The person can be involved in life story work, chronicling their life in detail and allowing their story to be shared and revisited as their memory deteriorates.

As the dementia progresses, the emphasis is on preserving the person's functioning for as long as possible, using favourite activities and strengths, behavioural techniques, reminiscence and reality orientation. Carers will need to develop strategies to minimise agitation, be able to deal with the behaviours that occur, and cope with delusions and hallucinations with reassurance, patience and redirection. Additional health needs must be dealt with as appropriate, especially the development of late onset epilepsy.

In the late stage, the pattern of care changes, with less emphasis on mental health and more emphasis on all aspects of physical health such as skin care, falls, mobility, posture, diet and swallowing. Professionals typically involved at this stage are nurses, physiotherapists, speech and language therapists (regarding swallowing), and dieticians.

Conclusion

Support staff have a vital role in providing care to older people with learning disabilities who have mental health problems. Flexibility in approach and knowledge of the issues will help staff to continue to care for people within their existing environments as they age. Familiarity and continuity are key to positive psychological well being in older age.

References and further reading

Department of Health (2001) *Valuing People: A New Strategy for Learning Disability for the 21st Century*. London: HMSO.

Dodd K, Turk V & Christmas M (2003) *Down's syndrome and dementia resource pack*. Kidderminster: British Institute of Learning Disabilities.

Fray MT (2000) *Caring for Kathleen: A Sister's Story about Down's Syndrome and Dementia*. Kidderminster: British Institute of Learning Disabilities.

Janicki MP & Dalton AJ (Eds) (1999) *Dementia, Ageing and Intellectual Disabilities: A Handbook*. Philadelphia: Brunner/Mazel.

Kerr D (1997) *Down's syndrome and dementia, A Practitioner's Guide*. Birmingham: British Association of Social Workers.

Patel D, Goldberg D & Moss S (1993) Psychiatric morbidity in older people with moderate and severe learning disability II: The prevalence study. *British Journal of Psychiatry* 163, 481–91.

Prasher VP (1995) Prevalence of psychiatric disorders in adults with Down syndrome. *European Journal of Psychiatry* 9, 77–82.

Prasher VP, Adams C, Holder R & Down Syndrome Research Group (2003) Long-term safety and efficacy of donepezil in the treatment of dementia in Alzheimer's disease in adults with Down syndrome: open label study. *International Journal of Geriatric Psychiatry* 18, 549–551.

Prasher VP, Huxley A & Haque M.S. (2002) A 24-week double blind, placebo-controlled trial of donepezil in patients with Down syndrome and Alzheimer's disease – Pilot study. *International Journal of Geriatric Psychiatry* 17, 270–278.

Sources of existing key resources/information

Dementia organisations

Alzheimer Society
10 Greatcoat Place
London
SW1P 1PH
Tel: 020 7306 0606

Learning disability organisations

BILD
Wolverhampton Road
Kidderminster
Worcs
DY10 3PP
Tel: 01562 850251

Down's Syndrome Association
155 Mitcham Lane
London
SW17 9PG
Tel: 020 8682 4001

Down's Syndrome Scotland
158/160 Balgreen Road
Edinburgh
EH11 3AU
Tel: 0131 313 4225

MENCAP
123 Golden Lane
London
EC1Y 0RT
Tel: 020 7454 0454

CHAPTER FOURTEEN

The mental health needs of children with learning disabilities

JEREMY TURK

Introduction

Children who have learning disabilities are at increased risk of being more:

- dependent on others for help in acquiring basic skills
- prone to physical difficulties
- prone to emotional and behavioural disturbance
- prone to social stigmatisation and its consequences.

Their families are at risk of:

- psychological difficulties in siblings and parents
- marital disharmony
- social isolation
- financial hardship.

Young people who have learning disabilities have multiple needs relating to:

- their learning disabilities
- their age
- the impact of their learning disabilities on the family.

Many services and professionals are usually involved in addressing the individual's special needs adequately, and in such a way as to promote as normal development as possible. Intervention is also required to prevent the development of *secondary handicaps* to which individuals may be more prone because of their learning disabilities, or lack of adequate social and educational provision (Turk, 1996a).

Children with learning disabilities are children at risk – from biological, psychological and social factors which interact – hence the need for intervention and support in all these areas.

Needs

The needs of a young person with learning disabilities include:

- medical
- emotional
- cognitive
- behavioural
- educational
- social
- familial.

Different services predominate in their contribution at different ages.

- Throughout **pre-school** years, health services undertake a major role involving paediatricians and child development teams. In some districts, jointly-funded multidisciplinary services provide educational and social input to pre-schoolers as well.

- In the **school years**, educational services undertake most support, whether in special schools for children with moderate or severe learning disabilities, or by means of extra input within mainstream classrooms, ensured by a 'full assessment' leading to a Statement of Educational Needs ('statementing'). This legal document outlines the child's educational needs and what special educational support is required to meet them. It can also list desirable health and social service inputs. A Statement ensures educational provision until 19 years of age (not just the usual age of 16).

- Thereafter, responsibility for individuals with learning disabilities falls mainly on social services. However, throughout childhood and adolescence there is continuous availability of specialist psychiatric and psychological services for young people, and occasionally highly specialised teams for young people with learning disabilities who have mental health problems. Also, further education courses ensure the availability of learning opportunities well into adulthood.

Multidisciplinary assistance

Essential components of helping a child with learning disabilities comprise:

1. medical
2. psychological
3. educational
4. familial
5. social
6. long term.

1. Medical

- Investigation of possible causes:
  - may have genetic counselling implications for individual and family
  - may highlight likely physical problems requiring intervention
  - may provide information on likely developmental and behavioural profiles and, thus, likely challenges to be faced (behavioural phenotype) (O'Brien, 2002; Turk & Sales, 1996).

- Evaluation and treatment of present medical conditions.

- Evaluation and treatment of sight or hearing (sensory) problems.

- Assessment for possible mental disorders found commonly in young people with learning disabilities:
  - autistic spectrum disorders (pervasive developmental disorders) (Lord & Bailey, 2002)

- hyperkinetic syndrome (attention deficit hyperactivity disorder) (Ramchandani *et al*, 2002).

- Assessment for, and treatment of epilepsy.

2. Psychological

- Encouragement of optimal development through:
  - comprehensive evaluation of individual profile of cognitive strengths and needs
  - early intervention programmes (eg Portage, EarlyBird).

- Evaluation of, and early intervention for, developing challenging behaviours (eg aggression, self-injury) by behavioural functional analysis and positive behaviour support.

- Counselling/psychotherapy (cognitive, behavioural, psychodynamic) for individual and/or family.

3. Educational

- Thorough evaluation of child's special educational needs.

- Completion of Statement in collaboration with individual, parents, local education authority and other involved professionals.

- Provision of education appropriate to individual's profile of strengths and needs.

- Regular review of appropriateness of provision.

- Availability of specialist services and support for classroom–based behavioural difficulties.

4. Familial (Turk, 1996b)

- Explanation of nature, chronicity and implications of child's learning disabilities to parents in simple terms.

- Facilitation of familial grieving, psychological adjustment and orientation towards future.

- Psychological and practical support for parents and siblings.

5. *Social*

- Welfare benefits.
- Respite care services.
- Holiday and leisure schemes.
- Parent and family support groups (such as MENCAP, 'syndrome societies').
- Contact-a-family.
- Share-a-family.

6. *Long term*

- Discussion with individual and family regarding accommodation, occupation, lifelong learning, care and support, self-expression and safety.

Prevalence

Emotional and behavioural difficulties are more frequent in children with learning disabilities than in their non-learning disabled peers. This is due to combinations of biological, psychological and social factors. The following percentages of children have been found to have an identifiable psychiatric disorder (Rutter *et al*, 1970)

- 7% of children in the general population
- 12% of children with a physical disorder or disability
- 33% of children with a brain dysfunction
- 50% of children with severe learning disabilities.

Causes of learning disabilities

It is important to distinguish between, and identify if at all possible:

- the cause of the child's long-term disability ('aetiology')
- the cause of the problem (such as challenging behaviour) which has triggered concern.

Information on aetiology for the individual and family is important because of:

- the individual's and family's basic right to know
- relief from uncertainty regarding the cause of the disabilities

- relief from the guilt that family and/or social factors were the cause of the learning disabilities or developmental or behavioural disturbance
- facilitation of grief resolution
- focusing towards the future
- essential genetic counselling where appropriate for the entire extended family
- instigation of interventions relevant to strengths and needs
- potential for identifying with and belonging to a support group.

Causes of emotional and behavioural problems in children and young people with learning disabilities

There are many causes of emotional and behavioural problems in young people with learning disabilities. Usually, several of these are responsible for the difficulties faced by any one child.

Constitutional

As with any young person, the individual's temperament will contribute substantially towards how the child reacts to experiences, and thus the nature and intensity of emotional or behavioural disturbance. Also, the presence of a specific genetic cause (such as fragile–X syndrome, Williams syndrome or Prader-Willi syndrome) will determine what developmental and behavioural challenges are likely to be encountered.

Medical

Behavioural disturbance may be caused by a medical condition, for example, diabetes or epilepsy. It may be a sign of physical discomfort in a child unable to communicate effectively, for example, severe pain due to heartburn, appendicitis or a fractured bone. Self-injury in the form of hitting the side of the head is a well–recognised presentation of middle ear infection (otitis media). Epilepsy can present as disturbed emotions and behaviour, even when full consciousness is maintained. Psychiatric disorder often presents with challenging behaviour. Although serious psychiatric conditions such as schizophrenia and manic depression are rare in children with learning disabilities, they are witnessed more often in this group than in children with average intellectual functioning. Brain damage may be a cause of both the learning disabilities and the behavioural disturbance. Medication can contribute as well.

Developmental

Behaviour may be appropriate for the developmental stage reached. It is often the *discrepancy* between the young person's progressing physical size, strength and motor skills, and their limited intellectual and social capacities, which creates problems.

Cognitive

It is not 'things' themselves which disturb us but the view we take of them. Thus, the reaction of others to the individual's disabilities is crucial, but so too is the reaction of the individual with learning disabilities to their own perception of the stigma associated with having disability, and their perceptions of other people's reactions. This explains why personal counselling and public education must always go hand in hand.

Familial

Emotional or behavioural disturbance in a young person with learning disabilities may be an understandable reaction to family tensions, psychopathology or expressed emotion. This may take the form of a reaction to persisting familial grief or chronic sorrow, or to parental anxieties regarding the past, present or future, or to conflict or inconsistency within the family.

Social

Problems may be understandable reactions to daily hassles and life events, persisting communication difficulties with associated frustration, social deprivation, abuse or neglect, bereavement, institutionalisation or infantilisation (being treated unnecessarily childishly).

Educational

Educational programmes which are pitched either too high or too low may contribute to emotional and behavioural disturbance, because of boredom or frustration and upset. The educational placement itself may be contributory. Learning with a disabled peer group may expose one to modelling on inappropriate and maladaptive behaviours. Conversely, learning with a more able group of classmates may highlight just how disabled children are to themselves, leaving them vulnerable to teasing, bullying, social isolation and low self-esteem.

Maladaptive learning

All of the above causes interact with the child's propensity to learn inappropriate and maladaptive responses to situations where there is a problem in gaining attention, avoiding social interaction or difficult tasks, or in getting one's own way.

Multidisciplinary interventions for problems encountered

Medical

Epilepsy can further aggravate learning disabilities and can cause, as well as exacerbate, behavioural problems. Its presence in association with severe learning disabilities is a potent vulnerability factor predisposing towards psychological difficulties. Anticonvulsant medication should be combined with psychological approaches.

Physical disfigurement may cause profound distress in the child and family, requiring long-term psychological support, and occasionally cosmetic treatment or reconstructive surgery.

Psychiatric disturbance may occasionally warrant medical intervention, such as the confirmed benefits of stimulant medication, such as methylphenidate (Ritalin) for hyperkinetic disorder (Pearson *et al*, 2004), selective serotonin reuptake inhibitors (SSRIs) for obsessive-compulsive features, depression and anxiety (Ziervogel, 2000) and melatonin for severe and intractable sleep disturbance (Turk, 2003).

Psychological

The impact on family functioning of the presence of a child with learning disabilities may be profound. This in turn may aggravate the child's problems. Thus, family therapy can be useful. Most often, behavioural approaches will be appropriate, although other family members will need to be included to act as co-therapists. Behavioural approaches are not without limitations, and this must be born in mind while devising and undertaking such interventions. Commonly experienced problems include:

- high response specificity to environment in which programme is undertaken with poor generalisation (ie improvement may not occur in different settings or with different individuals)

- need for long-term, intensive continuation of programme to maintain benefits and prevent relapse.

Educational

Special education, whether in special school or with specialist input in a mainstream school, is of primary importance in addressing the child with learning disabilities. Teaching programmes must be tailored to the child's developmental level and must be mindful of associated difficulties such as autism. This would require a particular emphasis on structured and predictable programmes, with a focus on the multiple qualitative impairments in social functioning, language and ritualistic tendencies which are the condition's hallmarks. Certain causes of learning disabilities may create specific requirements for classroom adaptations (for example the gaze aversion, sequential information processing difficulties and numeracy problems often witnessed in fragile-X syndrome) (Dew-Hughes, 2004).

Attention deficits

Attention deficits and overactivity are common in children with learning disabilities and are often consistent with the individual's developmental level. Sometimes they may be particularly marked (Seager & O'Brien 2003). There is evidence that certain genetic causes of learning disabilities are more likely to lead to these difficulties, for example, fragile-X syndrome, Smith–Magenis syndrome, tuberous sclerosis and Sanfillipo syndrome (Turk, 2004). The following features require consideration.

- **Inattentiveness**

  Is the child unable to concentrate for any length of time, even on enjoyed activities?

- **Restlessness**

  Is the child unable to stay seated for any length of time? Is he always up-and-down from his seat, even during mealtimes and other enjoyed activities?

- **Fidgeting**

  Is the child constantly twiddling his fingers and toes, and shuffling around on his bottom when seated?

- **Overactivity**

  Is the child always on the go?

- **Impulsiveness**

  Is he the sort of child who always acts first and thinks later – if at all? Is he unable to wait before doing something?

- **Distractibility**

  Even when he does concentrate, is this concentration extremely fragile so that even the slightest distraction breaks his concentration?

If all these features are present in a wide range of settings, irrespective of whom the child is with and what time it is ('all-pervasiveness') then the child may have hyperkinetic disorder (or attention deficit hyperactivity disorder). As well as requiring specialist educational and psychological input, individuals often benefit from stimulant medications such as methylphenidate. These must always be prescribed and monitored by experienced professionals who have undertaken a thorough and appropriate evaluation. Even children with severe learning disabilities can respond beneficially to concentration–enhancing approaches including stimulant medication.

Adolescence

Separation and individuation issues are particularly complex for adolescents with learning disabilities. The ongoing struggle between autonomy and dependency coexists with practical issues such as the development of sexual awareness and drives, and the need to ensure that individuals are protected from abuse and exploitation. Inability to achieve true independence from the family may be a cause of depression and anger.

Summary

Young people with learning disabilities have multiple special needs which include an increased likelihood of emotional and behavioural disturbance. Biological, psychological and social factors all interact and all require careful assessment and intervention, in order to maximise the child's welfare and minimise the risks of avoidable secondary handicaps. Inadequate knowledge, resources and support (practical and emotional) render young people with learning disabilities at risk of further distress and disadvantage. Close collaborative work by multiple agencies with the family throughout and beyond childhood is necessary to ensure optimal outcome.

References and further reading

Dew-Hughes D (2004) *Educating children with fragile X syndrome.* London: Routledge Falmer.

Foundation for People with Learning Disabilities (2002) *Count Us In: The report of the committee of inquiry into meeting the mental health needs of young people with learning disabilities.* London: Mental Health Foundation.

Lord C & Bailey A (2002) Autism spectrum disorders. In: M Rutter and E Taylor (Eds) *Child and Adolescent Psychiatry.* Oxford: Blackwell Science.

O'Brien G (2002) *Behavioural phenotypes in clinical practice.* London: MacKeith Press.

Pearson DA, Lane DM, Santos CW, Casat CD, Jerger SW, Loveland KA, Faria LP, Mansour R, Henderson JA, Payne CD, Roache JD, Lachar D & Cleveland LA (2004) Effects of methylphenidate treatment in children with mental retardation and ADHD: individual variation in medication response. *Journal of the American Academy of Child & Adolescent Psychiatry* 43, 686–98.

Ramchandani P, Joughin C & Zwi M (2002) Attention deficit hyperactivity disorder in children. *Clinical Evidence* 8, 280–290.

Rutter M, Graham P & Yule W (1970) *A neuropsychiatric study in childhood. Clinics in Developmental Medicine, No. 35/36.* London: Heinemann/Spastics International Medical Publications.

Seager MC & O'Brien G (2003) Attention deficit hyperactivity disorder: review of ADHD in learning disability. *Journal of Intellectual Disability Research* 47 (supplement 1), 26–31.

Turk J (1996a) Tertiary prevention of childhood mental health problems. In: T Kendrick, A Tylee & P Feeling (Eds) *The Prevention of Mental Illness in Primary Care.* Cambridge: Cambridge University Press.

Turk J (1996b) Working with parents of children who have severe learning disabilities. *Clinical Child Psychology & Psychiatry* 1, 583–598.

Turk J (2003) Melatonin supplementation for severe and intractable sleep disturbance in young people with developmental disabilities: short review and commentary. *Journal of Medical Genetics* 40, 793–796.

Turk J (2004) *The Contact a Family Directory – An introduction to behavioural phenotypes.* www.cafamily.org.uk/behaviou.html

Turk J & Sales J (1996) Behavioural phenotypes and their relevance to child mental health professionals. *Child Psychology & Psychiatry Review* 1, 4–11.

Ziervogel CF (2000) Selective serotonin reuptake inhibitors for children and adolescents. *European Child & Adolescent Psychiatry* 9 (supplement 1), 20–26.

CHAPTER FIFTEEN

Working with families

HELEN PHILP AND KIRIAKOS XENITIDIS

Introduction

When working with people with learning disabilities, it is often essential for professionals to be in frequent contact with their families. In comparison to other clinical fields, limited psychological research has been carried out with this service user group (Hatton *et al*, 1999). Historically, the simple fact of having learning disabilities has been considered an exclusion factor for any psychological intervention (Hollins & Sinason, 2000). The development of models of working with families over the last 20 to 30 years has gradually extended, however, to include families with individuals with learning disabilities. Placing an individual in their family context and considering the person's communication and relationships with their family facilitates a more holistic understanding of their level of functioning, needs and behaviour.

Individuals with learning disabilities are often dependent on family and carers throughout their lives. One or more parent may have dedicated much of their own life to the care of their son or daughter. Such dependency may raise a number of issues for the family. Families may experience feelings of loss and bereavement, both for their child and for their own personal expectations. Financial pressures may have been incurred through loss of earnings and increased childcare demands. Relationships may have been impacted, with overly close relationships developing between the person with learning disabilities and a carer, and possible distancing from other family members and/or a spouse.

In understanding some of the experiences of the family, we can endeavour to work supportively and in collaboration with families to facilitate improved relationships both with professionals and within the family.

In some situations, family therapy may be needed to address specific problems within the family; often, however, the involvement can occur on a more informal basis. Day-to-day contact between family members and the individual with learning disabilities may be facilitated by a support worker. The support worker has a crucial role in enabling individuals to maintain contact with family and friends, and to support them in coping with various issues as they arise.

The family as a 'system'

When we think of a family, we generally think of a group of 'related' people living together and sharing aspects of their life – the 'nuclear family'. We may also consider the 'extended family', and even close family friends. Each of these groups of people may be seen as a 'system' (see Chapter 4). The family can be seen as a dynamic system which co-evolves with its environment (Hoffman, 1982). The family is externally influenced by the environment, culture, society and other systems. Internally, the family is influenced by the development of family members and their relationships with one another as they progress through the life cycle (Hayes, 1991).

Specific external systems which may impact on our everyday lives include:

- educational systems
- work systems
- health systems
- religious systems
- local community systems
- culture.

Each of us will interact with some or all of these external systems at various points through life. For the individual with learning disabilities and their family, it is important to be aware of the extent to which these systems may have been influential in their lives. Families may have experienced systems as holding considerable control in decisions that might ordinarily have been made by the family alone (for example, the choice of mainstream or special school). This kind of influence and involvement may affect the ongoing relationships and trust that families experience when working with systems/authorities now. Often, external systems have an extensive role in the lives of people with learning disabilities. As doctors, nurses, social workers, teachers and support workers, we are all a part of these external systems. An awareness of our position and role within the family can allow us to be more effective in our support. It can be helpful in allowing us to gain information from the family and in supporting them in their relationships with one another.

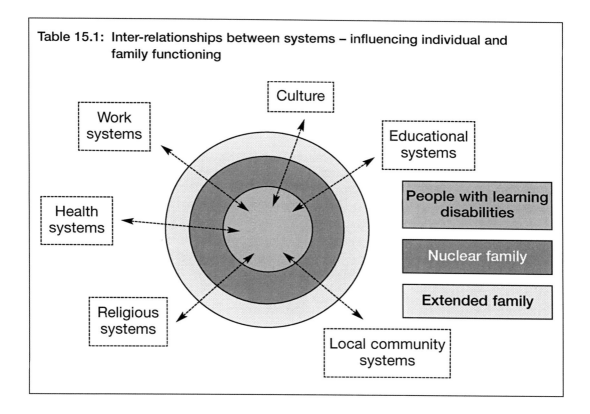

Table 15.1: Inter-relationships between systems – influencing individual and family functioning

Family therapy

Used in its broadest sense, family therapy refers to a treatment approach which 'looks at problems, within the system of relationships within which they occur, and aims to bring about change in the broader system rather than in the individual alone' (Burnham, 1986).

Families with a member with learning disabilities are likely to have tackled multiple difficulties over the years, with greater or lesser degrees of success. Family therapists might work with a family to address specific problems, for example, supporting the family through a particular difficulty or addressing behavioural problems. The family may offer vital information in understanding the behaviour.

Alternatively, families might have impacted on the development or maintenance of a problem, and therefore their inclusion is crucial in the successful treatment of the individual with learning disabilities.

Issues to be addressed within family therapy might include (Fidell, 2000):

- feelings of unresolved loss

- distorted life cycle transitions

- relationships with professional systems

- difficulties in attaining a balance between overprotection and autonomy of the adult with learning disabilities.

While these difficulties, and others, can benefit from family therapy intervention (Goldberg *et al*, 1995), a considerable amount of support can be successfully provided by support workers and carers during day-to-day interactions. We will consider these factors in greater detail later in the chapter.

There are a number of reasons for including the family when working with individuals with learning disabilities.

Many individuals with learning disabilities are dependent on their families for aspects of their care throughout childhood and continuing into adulthood. Often, it is the family that initiates contact with the learning disability services and/or mental health services, having identified problems or because they are no longer able to cope. It may be important to assess the family's attitudes towards, understanding of and expectations of both the individual and the services. These expectations may be unrealistic and/or it may be important to incorporate them in treatment.

Families may have struggled for many years to care for the person with learning disabilities. Acknowledging their commitment and listening to their experiences can be crucial in their engagement with services.

Families presenting an individual to learning disability and mental health services will have a perception of what they think the problem is and what they have observed. This could be crucial in understanding an individual's specific problem, especially as the person with learning disabilities may be less able to articulate this for themselves.

Families are often important contributors to the implementation and maintenance of treatment programmes, whether this includes compliance and monitoring of medication, or the implementation of a treatment programme to address challenging behaviour. Observation of side effects or active involvement in behaviour modification may all include the participation of the family.

The importance of carers has been acknowledged by recent government documents. The *National Service Framework for Mental Health* (NSF) (DH, 1999) sets standards for the access to services for all mental health needs, including assessment and provision of treatment (standard two) and for the assessment and provision of care to carers – 'caring about carers' (standard six).

The *NSF* also emphasises *The Carers (Recognition and Services) Act 1995*, which gives carers who provide 'substantial care on a regular basis' the right to request an assessment from social services.

The Government White Paper, *Valuing People* (DH, 2001) states the need to support carers. Within Government objectives for learning disability services, objective 4 states the requirement to increase the help and support received by carers from all local agencies in order to allow them to fulfil their family and caring roles effectively.

It is important to realise that the principles of family involvement are applicable not only to people living with their families but also to those living in group homes and other residential settings.

Life-cycle transitions

Our lives move through a number of stages. These may be defined by age (childhood > adolescence > adulthood > old age) and/or by life cycle transitional events (leaving school > marriage > birth of a child > launching a child > retirement).

Having learning disabilities is likely to have had a direct impact on many of the life-cycle transitions. The needs of a child with disabilities might result in the normal family decisions about school and involvement in family activities being more complex. In fact, what would normally be a private family decision about education might have been overridden by the advice or availability of appropriate educational facilities. Children might leave home at a young age to attend specialist residential schools while their siblings remain at home. Parents may feel disempowered, and children may feel 'different' and perhaps excluded from the family.

Conversely, in adult life, normal life-cycle transitions would support the child in 'flying the nest'. However, the young adult with learning disabilities might be unable to achieve this transition without the support of services.

Valuing People recognises this difficulty, setting as its second objective the need to ensure the continuity of care and support for the young person and their family. It promotes the need for equality in the provision of opportunities, enabling as many young people with disabilities as possible to participate in education, training or employment.

While services may address the practical needs of individuals and their families, it is also important that carers working with adults with learning disabilities should be sensitive to the experiences and associated emotions of leaving the family home and living in supported residential care. Gaining supported independence for the person with learning disabilities might have been a difficult transition for the individual and their family, and may be associated with feelings of anxiety, guilt or grief for the family, as well as raising new hopes and expectations.

Families may require support in renegotiating their relationships, perhaps after many years of dependency. Parents may now be free to pursue their own interests and re-establish a social network, something that they might have neglected for many years.

Grief and loss

Facilitating achievements is an important aspect of working with an individual with learning disabilities. We place a lot of emphasis on the importance of developing skills, increasing independence and, importantly, raising self-esteem. Sharing achievements with the family may be an important aspect within this process. It allows the inclusion of the family in life events and choices made by the individual, and may serve a valuable role in reinforcing independence and self-esteem.

In working with an individual with learning disabilities, there will have often been lengthy assessment procedures by psychologists, occupational therapists, nurses and support workers to ascertain the level of functioning of an individual, and thereby to allow us to plan our treatment interventions and day activities at an appropriate level. Sharing information from these assessments and the inclusion of the individual and their families in the planning of treatment is essential, not only because it ensures their involvement and choices, but also because it may also serve an important role in ensuring that individual, family and professional expectations are in synchrony.

Accepting the loss of 'what could have been' with a normal child (or what is often referred to as the 'perfect child' (Oswin, 1991)) may be an ongoing process for the family. Carers should be aware of the impact of family events – the marriage of a sibling or the birth of a child may be difficult reminders of unattained hopes for the person with learning disabilities. Increasing age and the possibility of the parents becoming ill may be sources of anxiety for the family.

Protection vs autonomy

The protection of an individual with learning disabilities is often an area of concern for both families and professionals. An individual may be striving for independence while their carers' view might be that they have inadequate skills/ coping strategies for a given situation, and are therefore vulnerable.

Parents might be perceived by professionals, their friends/peers or the person with learning disabilities as being overprotective. This can occur for a number of reasons (Goldberg *et al*, 1995):

• perceived vulnerability of the individual

• belief that the individual does not/is not able to fully understand a situation (eg coping with a bereavement)

• failure to cope in a given situation may result in a deterioration in behaviour or possible aggression

• protection from potential failure

• protection from the reality of learning disabilities

• recognition of one failure/loss may trigger recollection of past unresolved losses.

Individuals with learning disabilities are often thought to be particularly vulnerable in regard to relationships. Parents and carers may want to protect them because of:

• fear of pregnancy

• fear of exploitation

• uncertainty regarding the individual's understanding of relationships

• impact on the individual's behaviour if the relationship ends.

As professionals, we may participate formally in the protection of individuals with learning disabilities through the completion of risk assessment and management plans. Such procedures are seen as vital in ensuring the safety of a vulnerable adult.

Inclusion of the family in the risk assessment procedure may help to alleviate anxiety, while also allowing constructive evaluation with the family of their protective/overprotective role. Protection which may previously have been helpful may become overly restrictive and potentially disabling.

Carers must be cautious not to be critical of the protective parent but, rather, supportive and reassuring. Remember, there is a 'fine line' between protection and overprotection, and sometimes a good balance may be difficult to achieve.

Additional mental health problems

Families may have struggled for many years with the problems associated with living with an individual with learning disabilities. The additional problems incurred with mental illness might feel overwhelming.

Often, a major factor resulting in poor coping is a lack of understanding. Provision of information about the illness and the difficulties experienced by the individual with learning disabilities can be helpful in enabling the family to come to terms with a new diagnosis. Within community and residential settings, it is often the support worker with whom the family has most contact. Providing families with information may be achieved in a number of ways:

- supporting them in meeting with the psychiatrist
- provision of relevant literature
- informing them of relevant support groups:
    - National Schizophrenia Fellowship
    - National Autistic Trust
    - Mind
    - Mencap.

Allowing the family time to talk about their concerns can also help them to adjust. As we discussed earlier in this chapter, families can often have an important role in treatment compliance. Collaborative working with the family may therefore be valuable in the overall welfare of the person with learning disabilities.

Impact of learning disabilities on family relationships

In considering all the factors above, it is little wonder that more general family relationships are often affected. Having a family member with learning disabilities, and possible additional physical or mental health problems, often impacts financially, socially and emotionally on sibling and parental relationships. Families may have been excluded from social events, embarrassed by behaviours in public or financially restricted. Limitations on family life may have been such that they grieve their life before disability (Evans & Midence, 1999). Families may feel anger for this loss and/or guilty for this emotion. By the time the person with learning disabilities reaches adulthood, all of this might have been deeply buried by their family. It might be appropriate to encourage and support them (particularly the parents) to re-establish social contacts, and to spend time on social activities without always including the person with learning disabilities.

Summary

Families are often crucial in the lives and care provision of people with learning disabilities. While we must be aware of the need to maintain the rights and confidentiality of adult service users, the inclusion of the family can often enhance our understanding of both the service user's strengths and their difficulties. In developing an understanding of a person within context, we can hope to gain a better sense of their values and choices, and develop relationships and interventions that demonstrate a greater sensitivity to their personal, family and cultural preferences.

References and further reading

Burnham J (1986) *Family Therapy: First Steps towards a systemic approach*. London and New York: Routledge.

Department of Health (1999) *Mental Health: National Service Framework*. London: HMSO.

Department of Health (2001) *Valuing People: A New Strategy for Learning Disability for the 21st Century*. London: HMSO.

Evans A & Midence K (1999) Is there a role for family therapy in adults with learning disability? *Clinical Psychology Forum* 129, 30–33.

Fidell B (2000) Exploring the use of family therapy with adults with a learning disability. *Journal of Family Therapy* 22, 308–323.

Goldberg D, Magrill L, Hale J, Damaskinidou K, Paul J & Tham S (1995) Protection and Loss: working with learning disabled adults and their families. *Journal of Family Therapy* 17, 263–280.

Hatton C, Hastings R & Vetere A (1999) A case for inclusion? *The Psychologist* 12, 5.

Hayes H. (1991) A Re-introduction to Family Therapy – Clarification of Three Schools. *Australian and New Zealand Journal of Family Therapy* **12** (1) 27–43.

Hoffman L (1982) A Co-evolutionary Framework for Systemic Family Therapy. *Australian Journal of Family Therapy* 4, 9–21.

Hollins S & Sinason V (2000) Psychotherapy, learning disabilities and trauma: new perspectives. *The British Journal of Psychiatry* 176, 32–36.

Oswin M (1991) Am I allowed to cry? *The Study of Bereavement Amongst People with Learning Difficulties*. London: Souvenir Press.

CHAPTER SIXTEEN

Offenders with learning disabilities

KIRIAKOS XENITIDIS, MAX PICKARD, JAYNE HENRY AND NATALIE HISER

Introduction

The link between learning disabilities and offending behaviour is a complex one. Although there have been reports of increased frequency of offending among people with learning disabilities, it is generally agreed that there is no conclusive evidence of a general causal link between learning disabilities and a propensity to offend (Gunn & Taylor, 1993). Studies in this area are fraught with difficulties for a variety of reasons, including, importantly, the distinction between 'challenging' and 'offending' behaviour. There is little doubt that people with learning disabilities frequently commit what would normally be considered an offence. However, the combination of the relatively trivial nature of such offences and the presence of learning disabilities means that such behaviour is often not dealt with by the criminal justice system, and hence does not become a registered offence.

To be guilty of an offence requires two components: *Actus Reus* (that the act/crime was actually committed) and *Mens Rea* (literally 'guilty mind', or that the individual knew the act was wrong but wilfully committed it nevertheless). It is the second component of guilt, the *Mens Rea*, which is often called into question in people with learning disabilities, and in practice in its absence the offence(s) are labelled as 'challenging behaviour'.

This chapter will explore the relationship between learning disabilities and offending, and discuss ways in which people with learning disabilities who are offenders or at risk of offending can be helped to prevent offending.

How common is offending among people with learning disabilities?

Finding out how common offending is among people with learning disabilities is not straightforward. Research studies vary widely in their findings. This is mainly because of variation in terminology and case identification criteria.

In understanding the extent of the problem of offending behaviour in people with learning disabilities, it is important to keep in mind the different stages that the individual goes through in the criminal justice system. The pathway from offence to disposal is determined by the need to punish or treat the individual, and/or protect society. In most cultures and in most eras, the person with learning disabilities has been protected from the full vigour of the law, and this is true today. Under normal circumstances, this pathway would usually follow the following sequence:

1. The offence is committed.
2. The police are called and/or the offence is reported.
3. The police arrest the offender.
4. The police decide to prosecute.
5. The crown prosecution service decides to proceed with criminal proceedings.
6. The offender appears at court for pre-trial hearing (for remand).
7. The offender appears at court for trial and sentencing.

This is a very basic representation of this pathway and is not intended to capture the complexities of the criminal justice system, but simply to show the main stages of the process. People with learning disabilities can be diverted from this pathway at any of its stages. Victims or witnesses may be less willing to contact the police, the police (and criminal justice system) may decide that it is not in the public interest to prosecute, and the courts of law are likely to dispose of such cases in a less punitive manner. Hence, prevalence is expected to be higher at the earlier stages of the criminal justice system, and lower later on because of diversion policies.

One way of considering the relationship between offending and learning disabilities is by studying the prison, court and probation population, screening for learning disabilities. This method identifies offenders who have been through the criminal justice system, but it does not address the question of how often people with learning disabilities offend. Another way is to start with a sample of people with learning disabilities and ask which of them has a history of offending behaviour (McBrien, 2003). The rates of offending can then be compared to the general population of the same geographical area.

When screening a population, there is a wide variation in the different methods used to identify people with learning disabilities. The most commonly used ones are:

- **administrative:** those in contact with the learning disabilities services in an area or setting

- **special schooling:** this method assumes that responders who attended a special school will have the same difficulties when they become adults

- **self-reported reading and learning problems:** this is usually combined with questions regarding the type of school attended.

It would be ideal to use formal cognitive testing, resulting in an IQ score, for case identification. In a study by Clare & Gudjonsson (1992), 20% of people in police custody who had an IQ below 75 were only identified after formal IQ testing. However, this type of testing is resource-intensive, especially for large-scale studies. Furthermore, to take into account the definition of learning disabilities would mean to include measurements of adaptive behaviour (eg Mason & Murphy, 2002). This requires an informant and is not practical in prison and other criminal justice system settings. Systematic information on the prevalence of learning disabilities in prisons is scarce. It is likely, at least in the UK, that the incidence of learning disabilities in prisons is approximately 1% (Coid, 1988).

Offences committed by people with learning disabilities

It has to be remembered that a significant proportion of criminal offending is undetected or, if detected, remains unreported. On those occasions when the conviction stage is reached, most people with learning disabilities who are convicted, are convicted of acquisitive crimes, such as shoplifting. Examples of less common, but clearly more serious crimes committed by people with learning disabilities are violent crime, arson and sexual offences. When compared to offenders of average intellectual functioning, people with learning disabilities who have been convicted are more likely to be convicted of arson or sexual offences.

The process of being interviewed/interrogated by the police is generally stressful, and may be particularly so for people with learning disabilities. The Confait case threw light on the phenomenon of false confession, and this needs to be borne in mind. In this case, a boy with learning disabilities confessed to a crime he did not commit, in order to avoid cross-examination, and he was imprisoned wrongfully. This led to a report recommending the presence of an 'appropriate adult' in interview procedures when the person is thought to have learning disabilities (Royal Commission on Criminal Procedure, 1981).

In addition to being perpetrators of crime, people with learning disabilities can be witnesses of criminal behaviour. The following three situations are related to both the phenomenon of false confessions and the reliability of people with learning disabilities as witnesses of crime:

1. acquiescence (answering in the affirmative, regardless of the question)

2. suggestibility (believing a false proposition suggested to them)

3. compliance (compliance with what others say, even though they may not believe it).

Finally, people with learning disabilities are often victims themselves, of crimes perpetrated by their peers or, more often, by other people without learning disabilities. In these cases, their vulnerability needs to be taken into account as well as what has been called 'cycles of abuse', situations where the victim of a crime becomes a perpetrator of the same or similar crime. A typical example would be sexual offences committed by people with learning disabilities who have themselves been sexually abused.

Fitness to plead and stand trial

A key question in the process of court proceedings is the concept of fitness to plead and stand trial. Fitness to plead requires that the defendant is able to plead (ie make a plea of guilty or not guilty), comprehend the proceedings of the court and the evidence, instruct a solicitor, and challenge a juror. Fitness to plead is decided by the court, and solicitors may ask for an assessment by a psychologist or psychiatrist to advise the court. If the defendant is unfit to plead, the court proceeds with a trial of facts, which determines if the defendant committed the offence, but not if he or she is guilty. If the court finds the act was committed, it has a variety of disposals it can discharge, including admission to hospital for treatment, or probation orders with condition of treatment.

Special groups and conditions linked with learning disabilities

Autism

One of the characteristics of autism (including Asperger's syndrome) is a reduced or even absent ability to empathise, that is, to 'put oneself in another person's shoes'. As empathic sensibilities are an inhibitory factor in crimes, especially against a person, autism may be related to violent behaviour. Conversely, people with autism may be dogmatic and inflexible, and hence rigidly follow the letter of the law, which might be a protective factor. The relationship between autism and offending is not yet clear, although a number of individuals with autism do commit serious offences.

ADHD (attention deficit hyperactivity disorder)

This disorder is characterised by overactivity, impulsivity, and poor attention and concentration. It is often associated with behavioural problems on the one hand, and learning disabilities on the other. Although it is a condition typically manifested in childhood and tends to reduce in late teenage years, it sometimes persists into adulthood. One of the characteristics of ADHD is poor impulse control, which is a risk factor for offences. Childhood ADHD is linked to childhood conduct disorder which in turn is linked to adult personality disorder and criminality (Mannuzza *et al*, 1991).

Women offenders

A marked difference can be seen between the prevalence of crime among men and that among women in the general population. Over 90% of violent offences are committed by men. Female offenders show educational underachievement and lower than average intelligence scores. In a sample of 1272 randomly selected female offenders awaiting trial, severe cognitive impairment was found in five (0.4%) of the women (Teplin *et al*, 1996).

Brain damage

Because the definition of learning disabilities requires that the intellectual deficit occurs before the age of 18, those with IQ less than 70 because of brain damage in adult life do not technically have learning disabilities. However, brain damage in childhood or adolescence may be the cause of a person's learning disabilities. In addition, a number of people with learning disabilities may suffer brain damage as a result of accidents or epilepsy. Brain damage can affect behaviour (and thus precipitate offending) in a variety of ways including disinhibition, increased irritability, poor impulse control, reduced frustration tolerance and altered sexual behaviour.

Personality disorders

The relationship between personality disorder and learning disabilities is not clear and remains controversial. Although a discussion on this is beyond the scope of this chapter, it is clear that in the general population certain types of personality disorder, particularly the paranoid and/or dissocial types, are associated with criminality. In recent years there has been an increase in clinical and academic interest in the overlap between personality disorders and learning disabilities. (Flynn *et al*, 2002).

Substance misuse

The association between crime and substance misuse has been well established, both in the general population and in mentally disordered offenders in particular. Although alcohol and drug misuse is less common in people with learning disabilities in general, it is an important variable to keep in mind where offenders with learning disabilities are concerned. A recent study showed that over a quarter of offenders with learning disabilities had a history of alcohol or illicit drug misuse (Barron *et al*, 2004).

Epilepsy

Compared to the general population, people with learning disabilities are at higher risk of developing epilepsy. Epilepsy has been linked with offending behaviour. This can happen either as a result of 'automatic' behaviour during an epileptic seizure, or before or after a seizure (Fenwick,1990).

Treatment options

The treatment of offenders with learning disabilities, like the treatment of offenders in general, has followed the 'custody vs care' debate. Whether a person who breaks the law is in need of help or should be subjected to punishment has fuelled the debate over the years. Treatment is often made available under a legal framework, be that in hospital (*Mental Health Act 1983*), custody (prison–based therapeutic programmes) or community (probation with condition of treatment).

Drug treatments

The treatments available to people with learning disabilities and offending behaviour can be drug treatments (antidepressants, antipsychotics, antilibidinal drugs) or psychosocial interventions. Drug treatments are used to treat an underlying mental health problem (for example, a depressed woman who shoplifts), and are described elsewhere in this handbook. In addition, a specific category of medication, namely antiandrogens or antilibidinal medication, is used in the treatment of sex offenders, and aims at a reduction of their sex drive. This is usually used as an adjunct of a range of psychological treatments as described below.

Psychological treatment for offenders with learning disabilities

Although psychological assessment and treatment packages for mentally disordered offenders have been available for some time, it is only more recently that these have been adapted for use with offenders who have learning disabilities.

In order to be able to provide an appropriate treatment package, it is essential that a thorough assessment is carried out. This is particularly important in terms of risk. The assessment phase is crucial in gathering information from the individual and, importantly, from a range of sources, including family, previous carers, police, solicitors, social workers and other professionals. This allows for the development of an individual formulation, a process that brings together all the information in order to be able to hypothesise as to what factors may have contributed to the development of a particular problem, or in this case increased the risk of offending. Any treatment plan or intervention must be based on a formulation in order for it to be successful. The alternative is to provide one type of intervention for everybody without consideration of individual need, which would have a much lower chance of success. For example, if a formulation suggested that a young man was setting fires in order to communicate his feelings of powerlessness and helplessness, treatment focusing on assertiveness training would be much more appropriate than anger management work.

Currently, psychological treatment packages for offenders both with and without learning disabilities are most commonly based on a cognitive-behavioural approach (eg Lindsay, 2002). These can be offered on either an individual or a group basis. The latter is the preferred option in some cases (eg sex offender treatment programmes). Specific treatment packages have now been developed for people who commit specific offences such as sexual offences, arson and assault.

Sex offences

A sex-offender treatment programme is typically a group treatment facilitated by qualified therapists, lasting up to two years. Treatment components include sex education, emotional awareness, social skills, assertiveness, empathy, offending cycle, cognitive distortions and relapse prevention. Research studies have suggested that treatment can reduce re-offending (eg Lindsay *et al*, 1998) and that, following treatment, offenders are able to have increased community access (eg Xenitidis *et al*, 1999). Studies also report a reduction in attitudes consistent with sexual offending, and reductions in minimisation and denial of offences (Lindsay & Smith, 1998).

Arson

This programme is administered in an individual or group setting. Treatment components include functional analysis of fire setting, education about dangers of fire, interpersonal skills (social skills, assertiveness), emotion recognition and management (eg anger mangement), and relapse prevention. There is a dearth of studies regarding the outcome of treatment for adult arson offenders with learning disabilities. One study reported good outcome for individual cognitive and behavioural therapy (Clare *et al*, 1992). A more recent study found that, following group treatment for fire setting, offenders showed a reduction in fire interest and attitudes associated with fire setting, improved anger disposition and increase in self-esteem (Taylor *et al*, 2002).

Anger and aggression

Individual or group treatments, including cognitive-restructuring and self-instruction, arousal reduction, problem-solving, stress-inoculation and behavioural approaches have been used. Behavioural approaches have demonstrated good outcome in terms of a reduction of aggression (Whitaker, 2001). However, once the intervention is withdrawn, there is a likelihood that the aggression will reappear, since behavioural approaches do not focus on helping individuals to self-regulate behaviour. Individual case studies of cognitive behavioural treatment for anger with individuals with learning disabilities and seriously aggressive behaviour have shown good outcome in terms of reduction of aggression (Murphy & Clare, 1991).

Aside from these comprehensive treatment packages, clinical psychologists would also provide treatment not necessarily associated directly with a specific offence, but which were based on the formulation that they may increase the risk of re-offending (eg depression and/or anxiety). Furthermore, skills deficits can also be addressed through training packages for social skills and problem-solving skills.

Conclusion

People with learning disabilities are at risk of offending due to a number of factors, as outlined above. There is a need for offending behaviour among people with learning disabilities to be recognised as such, and followed through. Conversely, there is a need for increasing the awareness and identification of learning disabilities and associated conditions, within populations of offenders and in a variety of settings. Then the structures can be in place for the appropriate treatment options to be made available, thus preventing further offending.

References and further reading

Barron P, Hassiotis A & Banes J (2004) Offenders with intellectual disabilities: a prospective comparative study. *Journal of Intellectual Disability Research* 48, 69–76.

Clare ICH & Gudjonsson GH (1992) Devising and piloting an experimental version of the 'Notice to Detained Persons'. *The Royal Commission on Criminal Justice Research Study no 7*. London: HMSO.

Clare ICH, Murphy GH, Cox D & Chaplin EH (1992) Assessment and treatment of firesetting: a single case investigation using a cognitive behavioural model. *Criminal Behaviour and Mental Health* 2 253–268.

Coid J (1998) Mentally abnormal prisoners on remand – rejected or accepted by the NHS? *British Medical Journal* 296, 1779–182.

Department of Health (1983) *The Mental Health Act*. London: HMSO.

Fenwick P (1990) Automatism. In: M Bluglass and P Bowden (Eds) *Principles and Practice of Forensic Psychiatry*. London: Churchill Livingstone.

Flynn A, Matthews H & Hollins S (2002) Validity of the diagnosis of personality disorder in adults with learning disabilities and severe behavioural problems. *British Journal of Psychiatry* 180, 543–546.

Gunn J & Taylor P (1993) *Forensic Psychiatry: Clinical legal and ethical issues*. Oxford: Butterworth-Heinemann.

Lindsay WR (2002) Research and literature on sex offenders with intellectual and developmental disabilities. *Journal of Intellectual Disability Research* 46, (Supplement I) 74–85.

Lindsay WR, Neilson C, Morrisson F & Smith A (1998) The treatment of six men convicted of sex offences. *British Journal of Clinical Psychology* 37, 83–98.

Lindsay WR & Smith A (1998) Responses to treatment for sex offenders with intellectual disability: a comparison of men with 1 and 2 year probation sentences. *Journal of Intellectual Disability Research* **42** (5) 346–353.

Mannuzza S, Klein RG, Bonagagura N, Malloy P, Giampino T & Addalli KA (1991) Hyperactive children almost grown up. *Archives of General Psychiatry* 48, 77–83.

Mason J & Murphy G (2002) Intellectual disability amongst people on probation: prevalence and outcome. *Journal of Intellectual Disability Research* **46** (3) 230–238.

McBrien J (2003) The Intellectually disabled offender: Methodological problems in identification. *Journal of Applied Research in Intellectual Disabilities* 16, 95–105.

Murphy GH & Clare ICH (1991) MIETS: A service option for people with mild mental handicaps and challenging behaviour or psychiatric problems. Assessment, treatment and outcome for service users and service effectiveness. *Mental Handicap Research* 4, 180–206.

Royal Commission on Criminal Procedure (1981) *Report of the Royal Commission on Criminal Procedure*. London: HMSO.

Taylor J, Thorne I, Robertson A & Avery G (2002) Evaluation of a group intervention for convicted arsonists with mild and borderline intellectual disabilities. *Criminal Behaviour and Mental Health* 12, 282–293.

Teplin LA, Abram KM & McClelland GM (1996) Prevalence of psychiatric disorder among incarcerated women. *Archives of General Psychiatry* 53, 505–512.

Whitaker S (2001) Anger control for People with Learning Disabilities; A Critical Review. *Behavioural and Cognitive Psychotherapy* **29** (3) 277–293.

Xenitidis KI, Henry J, Russell AJ, Ward A & Murphy DG (1999) An inpatient treatment model for adults with mild intellectual disability and challenging behaviour. *Journal of Intellectual Disability Research* **43** (2) 128–134.

CHAPTER SEVENTEEN

Cultural diversity, mental health and learning disabilities

RAGHU RAGHAVAN AND JEAN O'HARA

Introduction

This chapter will explore cultural diversity and its significance in planning services for, and delivering care to, people from Black and minority ethnic communities with learning disabilities and mental health problems, and their families.

Britain is a multicultural society, where we live side by side with people from different ethnic, cultural, social and religious backgrounds. It is estimated that nearly 6.4 million people in England belong to minority ethnic communities. This consists of people from Irish communities, Afro Caribbean communities, South Asians (normally referred to as the Indian subcontinent – referring to people from India, Pakistan, Bangladesh and Sri Lanka) and the Chinese community. Refugees and asylum seekers from the former Eastern European countries are also considered as minority ethnic communities.

Although people from Black minority and ethnic (BME) backgrounds have been present in large numbers in the UK since the second world war (including people from Africa, South Asia, the Caribbean, Ireland, Poland and Ukraine), research in the last two decades shows that many of these people face inequalities, discrimination and disadvantage in our society. People from BME groups form a significant part of the UK population, about 4.6 million people (7.9% of the population) in the 2001 census (www.statistics.gov.uk), and 50% live within the Greater London area.

Assuming a 2% prevalence rate for learning disabilities (probably a considerable underestimate for BME communities), this means there will be 92,000 people with learning disabilities from BME communities in the UK. We are currently seeing a steady rise of people from diverse cultures and religious beliefs in Europe and other western countries such as the USA and Canada. It is important that we understand the prevalence and meaning of learning disabilities within their cultures in order to adequately meet their needs.

The UK Government's White Paper, *Valuing People* (Department of Health, 2001) highlights that the needs of people with learning disabilities from minority ethnic communities are often overlooked. The key issues involve a high prevalence of learning disabilities in some minority ethnic populations, social exclusion and a lack of understanding of the significance of cultural and religious beliefs of family carers.

What is culture?

Historically, the word 'culture' has been used to describe many aspects of social life. Helman (2001) describes culture as a set of guidelines (both implicit and explicit) that individuals inherit as members of a particular society, which informs them how to view the world, how to experience it emotionally, and how to behave in it in relation to other people, to supernatural forces and Gods, and to the natural environment.

Hall (1984) proposed three different levels of culture:

* the **tertiary** level of culture – the explicit manifestation of culture visible to the outsider, such as social rituals, traditional dress, national cuisine and festive occasions

* the **secondary** level of culture – the implicit assumptions, beliefs and rules which constitute the 'cultural grammar' of the group

* the **primary** level of culture – the deepest level of culture, in which the rules are known to all and obeyed by all, although this is seldom stated.

Cultural background has a significant influence on many aspects of people's lives, and includes their beliefs, behaviour, perceptions, emotions, language, religion, rituals, family structure, diet, dress, body image, concepts of space and time, and attitudes to illness, pain and other forms of misfortune (Helman, 2001).

Ethnicity

Ethnicity is a common term used in health and social sciences, and definitions of it include references to place of origin or ancestry, skin colour, cultural heritage, religion and language. Ethnicity is defined by the individual as his/her sense of psychological belonging. This sense of belonging is dynamic. It may change with time and with individual experiences. An individual may feel they belong to an ethnic group as a result of certain shared characteristics including ancestral and geographical origins, social and cultural traditions, religion and languages (Mackintosh *et al*, 1998).

It is important to understand that we all belong to ethnic groups, even though the term 'ethnic' is often incorrectly used only to refer to individuals from black and minority backgrounds.

Race

The term 'race' originated in relation to assumed biological differences between particular groups sharing certain distinguishing physical characteristics, such as bone structure and skin colour (Giger & Davidhizar, 1999). However, we now know through population and genetic studies that there is little genetic deference between the various racial groups, and hence the term 'race' has been discredited. *The Parekh Report* (Runnymede Trust, 2000) argues that race is a social and political construct, and not a biological or genetic fact.

Cultural diversity

Cultural diversity encompasses issues of perceived and real differences with respect to age, gender, ethnicity, disability, religion, lifestyles, family and kinship, dietary preferences, traditional dress, language or dialects spoken, sexual orientation, educational and occupational status, and other factors (Purnell & Paulanka, 1998). In valuing diversity and being aware of diversity, an understanding of values, beliefs, behaviours and orientations is essential.

Black and minority ethnic population and mental health

It is well documented that BME communities face inequalities in mental health care (NIMHE, 2003; DH, 2005). For example, people from these communities are more likely to be:

- detained under the *Mental Health Act 1983* and the *Mental Health Act (Scotland) 1984*

- diagnosed as suffering from schizophrenia or other forms of psychotic illness

- detained in locked wards

- regarded as 'dangerous' and treated accordingly, often leading to over-representation in secure settings.

In terms of service access and appropriateness, people from BME communities face significant difficulties. For example:

- alternatives to hospital admission are less likely to be offered to minority ethnic communities

- offers of talking therapies such as psychotherapy and counselling are restricted

- there is a failure to recognise and accept concepts of mental health from other cultures

- there is a failure to take account of the effects of racism, discrimination or perceived discrimination and socio-economic factors on a person's mental health

- the stigmatising effect of using conventional psychiatric inpatient services in these communities is not adequately recognised.

Black and minority ethnic population and learning disabilities

The population census indicates a growing population of BME communities in the UK. It is suggested that the prevalence of learning disabilities among UK South Asian communities may be up to three times higher than other communities (Azmi *et al*, 1996), and the Pakistani and Bangladeshi community population may be more affected than the Indian communities. There is very little information about the prevalence of learning disabilities in other minority ethnic communities such as Afro-Caribbean and Chinese populations. Research also suggests an over-representation of children from minority ethnic groups in special education, compared to their white peers (Hatton *et al*, 2002). Residential services show an under-representation of people with learning disabilities from minority ethnic groups, and evidence also suggests an under-representation of South Asian adults from the UK using psychiatric services. Although GP consultation rates are higher in south-east Asian communities compared to their white peers, there is less awareness of the existence of specialist services, and there is a danger that carers' psychological and emotional distress continues to go unrecognised. The burden of care is therefore greater, because families are often isolated, and living in poverty and social deprivation.

A recent review of cultural diversity and learning disabilities studies highlights these experiences of stigma, isolation and racism as well as the creation of social barriers, negative attitudes of professionals and a lack of cultural sensitivity in service delivery (Raghavan & Small, 2004).

In fact, the whole process of labelling someone as being either mentally ill or learning disabled is culture-bound to a certain extent. Symptoms and behaviours are interpreted by professionals and compared against a cultural 'norm'. The definition of learning disabilities can be considered to be a social construct with arbitrary measures of intellectual and social functioning. Psychometric tests have a cultural bias.

Key issues

The key issues affecting people with learning disabilities and their families from BME communities are:

- a 'colour-blind' approach, where services are offered on the same basis to all communities. It ignores cultural strengths and fails to acknowledge that service provision is geared towards the dominant white majority culture, ignoring the needs of minority ethnic communities and the barriers that they face in accessing the services. This results in lack of attention to meeting the needs of BME communities and the lack of any mechanisms to explore and address their needs.

- Socio-economic deprivation – many families from BME communities live in inner city areas and many of these families experience material disadvantage in terms of housing, employment, income and benefits.

- Stereotyped opinions held by service planners and providers (such as of South Asian families 'looking after their own') will only isolate South Asian carers, and prevent them from expressing a contrary opinion about services. Another example is the stereotyped view of African Caribbean communities as impoverished, threatening and in need of control, which also serves to isolate people from these communities in planning services.

- Families from BME communities with disabled children commonly face simultaneous or additional barriers to equal opportunities and treatment, compared to parents from the majority population, because of discrimination or perceived discrimination in service provision and from professionals.

- Institutional and structural racism, both intentional and often unintentional, affects care, and results in poor material circumstances and low access to appropriate services.

- Awareness of services – many families are not aware of the services available for people with learning disabilities with challenging behaviour and/or mental health problems. As a result, the uptake of specialist services and specialist support services (such as speech and language therapy, psychology) is very low.

- Language barriers – a key factor in the uptake of services is language and communication. Many families are unable to communicate fluently using the English language, and hence their views are not heard. Even where families are able to speak English, poor communication between the family and the service provider creates barriers in terms of opportunities for discussing concerns and appraising options for care or support.

- Religious and cultural beliefs – for many South Asian families, religion is fundamental to how they live their lives. The importance of faith and prayer in accepting, understanding and treating mental illness may be given a strong focus in these communities. Although there is a wide variation in the extent to which the 'younger generation', mostly born in the UK, maintain traditional practices, gender roles, family obligations and religious observances, more than 50% of young people with learning disabilities from this community reported active observance of their religion (Azmi *et al*,1997). Many more felt they were treated badly because of their ethnic group. Slightly fewer felt they were treated badly because of their disability.

- Families from BME communities experience severe stress and trauma in caring for the young or older person with learning disabilities. Sometimes the families have to care for more than one person with learning disabilities, which is common in the South Asian community. As a result, they may be at particular risk of poor physical and mental health.

- Complex ethnicity, disability and mental health issues interact with one another, leading to increased risk of developing mental ill health in people with learning disabilities from BME communities (O'Hara, 2003).

Developing culturally sensitive services

Acheson Report

The *Acheson Report* (Health of Londoners Project, 1999) into inequalities in health recommends an increase in 'cultural competency' on the part of service providers and suggests that greater sensitivity and response to the needs of minority ethnic communities is required to overcome the disadvantages that they face (Mir *et al*, 2001). In creating a culturally sensitive service, it is essential that commissioners and service providers have a clear understanding of the needs of diverse and minority ethnic communities in their locality. It is essential that commissioners and service providers have the willingness and motivation to work in partnership with BME communities in shaping the landscape of services for people with learning disabilities with mental health problems.

The essential factors contributing to the development of culturally sensitive services consist of:

- establishing links between statutory, voluntary and private sector service providers and the BME communities; this should

  - not be seen as a mere 'tokenism' of consultation, but as an opportunity to build bridges with minority communities in exploring their views, opinions and needs in developing inclusive services

  - involve formal links with these communities at both collective and individual levels, in estimating the needs of people with learning disabilities from these communities.

  - include partnership working as integral to the service planning process

- consultation with BME communities to increase the awareness of the workforce and to develop sensitivity to the circumstances of these communities

- appropriate and adequate training for the workforce of the needs of BME communities and, more importantly, for building a culture of anti-discriminatory practices

- building confidence about services in BME families; this is vital in creating culturally sensitive services, and should:

  - involve active listening to the needs of the community and exploring ways in which services can best address these needs

  - be a continuous (rather than a snapshot) process, engrained in the service strategy, involving all sections of the community

- appropriate and adequate information of services available in the locality and nationally, in language that is appropriate and acceptable to BME communities; this should involve not only written materials explaining the nature of services and contact details but also audio visual resources (such as audio and video tapes) for people who may not be able to read

- developing appropriate support networks for people with learning disabilities and their families from BME communities (this may take the form of support groups of people with learning disabilities and carers' groups, which will help with the decision making process and an increase in participation and control)

- introducing liaison workers to broker appropriate services with family carers and service sectors. (A recent study in Bradford (Raghavan *et al*, in press) suggests positive outcomes for the young people and satisfaction by the family carers when a liaison worker is present to support the mental health needs of young people from Pakistani and Bangladeshi communities.)

References and further reading

Azmi S, Hatton C, Emerson E & Caine A (1997) Listening to adolescents and adults with intellectual disability in South Asian communities. *Journal of Applied Research in Intellectual Disability* 10, 250–263.

Azmi S, Hatton C, Caine A & Emerson E. (1996) *Improving Services for Asian People with Learning Disabilities.* Manchester: Hester Adrian Research Centre/Mental Health Foundation.

Bhui K & Bhugra D (2004) Communication with patients from other cultures: the place of explanatory models. *Advances in Psychiatric Treatment* 10, 474–478.

Department of Health (2001) *Valuing People: A New strategy for Learning Disability for the 21st Century.* London: HMSO.

Department of Health (2005) *Delivering race equality in mental health care: An action plan for reform inside and outside services and the Government's response to the Independent inquiry into the death of David Bennett.* London: HMSO.

Giger JN & Davidhizar RE (1999) *Transcultural Nursing: Assessment and Intervention.* St.Louis: Mosby.

Hall ET (1984) *The Dance of Life.* New York: Anchor Press.

Hatton C, Akram Y, Shah S, Robertson J & Emerson E. (2002) *Supporting South Asian families with a child with severe disabilities: A report to the Department of Health.* Lancaster University, Institute of Health Research.

Health of Londoners Project (1999) *Acheson Report: The Inquiry into Inequalities in Health: Implications for London – a discussion paper.* London: Department of Public Health, East London & The City Health Authority.

Helman CG (2001) *Culture, Health and Illness.* London: Arnold.

Mackintosh J, Bhopal R, Unwin N & Ahmad N (1998) *Step by step guide to epidemiological health needs assessment for minority ethnic groups.* Newcastle: University of Newcastle.

Mir G, Nocon A, Ahmad W & Jones L (2001) *Learning Difficulties and Ethnicity.* London: Department of Health, HMSO.

National Institute for Mental Health in England (NIMHE) (2003) *Inside outside: Improving Mental Health Services for Black and Minority Ethnic Communities in England.* Leeds: NIMHE.

O'Hara J (2003) Learning disabilities and ethnicity: achieving cultural competence. *Advances in Psychiatric Treatment* 19 166–174.

Purnell LD & Paulanka BJ (1998) *Transcultural Health Care: A culturally competent Approach.* Philadelphia: FA Davies.

Raghavan R, Small N, Newell R & Waseem F (In press) *Self-defined Service Models for Young People with Learning Disabilities and Mental Health Needs from Minority Ethnic Groups.* London: Foundation for People with Learning Disabilities.

Raghavan R & Small N (2004) Cultural diversity and intellectual disability. *Current Opinion in Psychiatry* 17, 371–375.

Runnymede Trust (2000) *The Future of Multi-Ethnic Britain – The Parekh report.* London: Profile Books.

CHAPTER EIGHTEEN

Evaluation of mental health training for carer staff supporting people with learning disabilities

HELEN COSTELLO

Introduction

Carers play a central role in the identification and assessment of mental health problems in individuals with learning disabilities. Yet, there is evidence to suggest that carers lack the skills to perform this role (Borthwick-Duffy & Eyman, 1990; Moss & Patel, 1993; Piachaud, 1999) and it is estimated that there are many people with learning disabilities who have undetected mental health problems (Reiss, 1993). This has negative consequences for the quality of life of individuals with learning disabilities and their carers, and for the costs and quality of services provided in community settings.

Given the high prevalence of mental health problems and the relatively low utilisation of mental health services by individuals with learning disabilities, documenting obstacles on the pathway to care and evaluating initiatives aimed at increasing access to services are research priorities. While it is often suggested that training may help to improve the sensitivity and accuracy of the case recognition and referral process (Moss, 2000; Holt, *et al*, 2000b) evidence about the effectiveness of mental health training is rarely reported.

This chapter describes the evaluation of a series of training workshops using selected modules from an earlier edition of the *Mental Health and Learning Disabilities* training package (Bouras & Holt, 1997). The chapter examines carer awareness of mental health problems in the absence of training, and presents evidence to suggest that training may improve knowledge of psychopathology, attitudes towards mental health services and practice. The implications of these results for the provision of training initiatives are discussed.

The 'Mental Health and Learning Disabilities' training workshop

This introductory workshop is one of a range of training courses provided by the Estia centre, and is a training and research resource specialising in the mental health of people with learning disabilities. The workshop is designed for family carers and direct care staff working in community day, residential and respite settings for individuals with learning disabilities. The broad aims of the workshop are to raise awareness of mental health issues, to increase understanding of the mental health needs of the people with learning disabilities and to explore how these needs can be assessed and subsequently met. Emphasis is therefore on the introduction of a range of issues influencing the mental health of individuals with learning disabilities rather than specific skills training and practice.

The workshop uses materials from two modules in *Mental Health and Learning Disabilities* (Bouras & Holt, 1997): 'Emotional Disorders' and 'Assessment of Mental Health Needs'. Workshops are delivered by an experienced training co-ordinator, each lasting for seven hours and divided into seven sessions focusing on different aspects of mental health problems. Session topics and learning objectives are summarised in **Table 18.1**. The video 'Making Links' (Holt & Bouras, 1997), which accompanies the training package, was used as the basis for Session 4 (Video case studies).

Table 18.1: Training topics & learning objectives	
Training session and topic	Learning objective
Session 1: Differences between mental health problems & learning disabilities	• Awareness that people with learning disabilities may suffer from a mental illness
Session 2: Common mental health problems & manifestation in people with learning disabilities	• Ability to identify the most common types of mental health problem • Awareness of patterns of behaviour and mood associated with possible mental illness
Session 3: Vulnerabilities of people with learning disabilities to developing mental health problems	• Understanding of why people with learning disabilities are vulnerable to developing mental health problems
Session 4: Video case studies	• Understanding of staff role in the identification, referral and assessment process
Session 5: The role of the multi-disciplinary team	• Basic understanding of the role of the multi-disciplinary team • Awareness of bio-psycho-social context of mental health • Awareness of how to obtain and work with specialised mental health services
Session 6: Medication and treatment options	• Basic understanding of common medicines and treatment options
Session 7: Summary session	• Summary of learning objectives

Evaluation of the training workshop

Carer knowledge, attitudes and beliefs about challenging behaviours are important influences on carer responses when such behaviours occur. For example, carer understanding of why behaviours occur determines the likelihood of external opinions being sought (Hastings & Remington, 1994) and determines the probability of advice given by peers, professionals or managers being effectively implemented

(Woods & Cullen, 1983; Emerson & Emerson, 1987). Given the overlap between the manifestation of mental health problems and challenging behaviour (Emerson *et al*, 1999; Rojahn *et al*, 1993; Walshe *et al*, 1993), it is highly probable that many of the factors determining carer responses to challenging behaviour are also applicable to the presence of mental health problems.

As such, carer knowledge, attitudes and beliefs may constitute important training resources for shaping behaviour towards individuals with learning disabilities and mental health problems. For example, improving knowledge about the behaviours associated with mental health problems may enable carers to recognise symptoms more accurately and to make informed decisions about when to refer a person for further assessment. Likewise, information about the role of mental health services and about therapeutic options may help to dispel myths and prejudices and make services more accessible. At a diagnostic level, greater insight into the types of behaviours pertinent to psychiatric assessment enables carers to provide better quality information to GPs and mental health professionals.

As part of a larger study evaluating the outcomes of training, carers attending the 'Mental Health and Learning Disabilities' workshop were asked to complete a self-report measuring awareness of mental health problems in people with learning disabilities. This comprised 15 statements relating to three aspects of awareness:

1. knowledge of psychopathology (5 items)

2. attitudes towards mental health services (5 items)

3. practice in relation to those behaviours associated with mental health problems (5 items).

Carers indicated 'agree', 'disagree' or 'don't know'. Correct responses were scored 1 and added to generate a total awareness score ranging from 0 to 15. There were also subscale scores for knowledge, attitudes and practice, ranging from 0 to 5. Sociodemographic data, such as age, gender and tenure were also recorded.

The questionnaire was completed immediately before training and four months after it. In this way, it was possible to measure whether training led to significant increases in carer awareness, and whether it was sustained over a four-month period. A comparison group was drawn from residential learning disability services in a neighbouring district. This group did not receive training, but completed the awareness questionnaire on two occasions, four months apart.

A total of 12 workshops were conducted and 66 care staff received training. The response rate was 83%. The majority were female (56%) with an average age of 37 (SD± 10.3). The comparison group comprised 65 care staff (response rate 87%)

and the only difference in the characteristics of the two groups related to tenure, with those carers in the comparison group having worked significantly longer in the learning disability services (an average of 96 months versus 52 months).

Awareness of mental health problems in the absence of training

Knowledge of psychopathology

This section of the questionnaire comprised statements describing the occurrence and manifestation of mental health problems in individuals with learning disabilities. Taking the two groups as a whole (n=131), prior to training the majority of carers agreed that there was a difference between learning disabilities and mental health problems (72%), and they were aware that individuals with learning disabilities were more vulnerable than the general population to developing mental health problems (75%) and that they could suffer from depression (89%). However, carers were inadequately informed about the range of behaviours indicative of mental health problems in individuals with learning disabilities. Less than half of the carers were aware that mental health problems may manifest in challenging behaviour (44%) and knew the prevalence range of mental health problems in this population (36%).

Attitudes towards mental health services

These statements examined carer attitudes towards the mental health services, about the role of mental health professionals and about their role in identifying and assessing mental health problems. The majority agreed that psychiatric interventions extended beyond drug therapy (77%), that psychiatric assessment incorporates both physical and social needs (67%) and that carers had a special role to play in the detection of mental health problems (71%). However, almost half of the staff believed that individuals with learning disabilities had enough labels without a psychiatric diagnosis as well (48%) and most staff were not aware of what type of information was required in order to assess mental health (60%).

A lack of understanding of the benefits of interventions by mental health services may lead to misgivings about approaching services, and represents a significant barrier in the referral of individuals with potential mental health problems to services. Also, the majority of staff lacked the necessary information required to fulfil what they considered to be an important aspect of their work. This has serious implications for staff confidence and competence in meeting the mental health needs of individuals in their care and in making appropriate referrals to services. At the same time, approximately one quarter of care staff disagreed that the detection of mental health problems was part of their job role.

Practice towards mental health problems

These statements described a behaviour associated with mental health problems and a possible carer response, such as making an appointment with the GP. In common with previous research (Edelstein & Glenwick, 1997, 2001; Spengler *et al*, 1990), the findings highlight the importance of the nature of symptoms exhibited. The majority of carers indicated that that they would seek advice if the person they supported suddenly began to talk to him- or herself (77%) or if the person kept bursting into tears (62%). However, fewer than half of the carers indicated that they would seek external advice in response to three-hour-long daily handwashing (41%), social withdrawal (33%) and early waking (46%). Hence, carers were less likely to agree that further assessment was appropriate if behaviours were inconspicuous and less disruptive. This finding provides further evidence that while carers may be aware of the presence of the behaviours associated with mental illness, they are unaware of their clinical significance and the need for treatment.

Awareness of mental health problems following training

Table 18.2 shows the total awareness score and subscale scores for knowledge, attitudes and practice before and after training for the intervention group, and at baseline and four months later for the comparison group. Mann Whitney U tests showed no significant differences between the groups in respect of the baseline total scores (U=2114, Z=-.144, p=.885) and subscale scores for knowledge (U=2029.5, z=-.553, p=.580), attitudes (U=2054.50, Z=-.432, p=.666) and practice (U=1955, Z=-.899, p=.369).

Awareness scores (median and range)	Intervention group		Comparison group	
	Baseline (n=66)	Follow-up (n=45)	Baseline (n=65)	Follow-up (n=59)
Knowledge	3.00 (0–5)	4.00 (0–5)	3.00 (1–5)	3.00 (1–5)
Attitudes	3.00 (1–5)	4.00 (1–5)	3.00 (0–5)	3.00 (0–5)
Attributions	2.00 (0–5)	3.00 (1–5)	3.00 (0–5)	3.00 (0–5)
Total score	9.00 (3–15)	12.0 (5–15)	8.00 (3–15)	9.00 (5–14)

Table 18.2: Awareness scores for the intervention group and comparison group at baseline & follow-up

The results indicate that the total and subscale awareness scores for the intervention group increased as a function of training. Following training, total awareness scores increased from 9 to 12, significantly higher than that attained by the comparison group at follow-up ($U = 736.00$, $Z=-6.04$, $p<.001$). Wilcoxon signed rank tests indicated significant increases between baseline and follow-up for total awareness scores ($Z=-5.105$, $p<.001$) and for subscale scores for knowledge ($Z=-3.190$, $p=.001$), attitudes ($Z=-3.504$, $p<.001$).and practice ($Z=-3.504$, $p<.001$). Analysis showed no significant changes over the same time period in total and subscale scores for the comparison group.

Bivariate correlations were conducted between changes in awareness scores and a range of independent variables (staff age, tenure, stress and coping strategies). Pearson's correlation coefficient indicated an inverse, but moderate, relationship between changes in awareness scores and staff age ($r=-.286$, $p=.020$). This suggests that greater changes in awareness scores were associated with lower staff age. Therefore, younger staff exhibited the greatest improvements in awareness, following training.

Implications for further training and research

In the absence of training, carers achieved relatively high total and subscale awareness scores. However, confirming previous research (eg Quigley *et al*, 2001), examination of the individual questionnaire items revealed a number of inadequacies in staff awareness. This supports the need for training interventions for staff working in community services for people with learning disabilities. This implies providing information about the range of associated behaviours and about the availability and efficacy of mental health services and interventions. This will increase staff understanding about their role in the identification and assessment process, and reduce potential barriers in the referral process. The provision of training is also instrumental in improving the detection of mental health problems by ensuring that carers consider its presence as one of the many possible causes of problem behaviours in individuals with learning disabilities.

The study found evidence to suggest that a brief training workshop was successful in improving carer awareness of mental health problems and that these gains were still evident four months after the delivery of training. Following training, care staff had increased knowledge about psychopathology and more positive attitudes towards mental health services, and were more likely to indicate that referral was appropriate in response to the behaviours associated with mental health problems. This training workshop could be readily adopted by service providers to deliver in-house training and the results suggest that this could improve staff ability to recognise and refer individuals with mental health problems. The finding that younger staff gained the greatest increases in awareness warrants further investigation and may indicate the added value of specifically targeting this group.

A number of limitations in the evaluation merit further discussion, namely that the random allocation to study groups was not possible. This may have resulted in a number of potentially important unmeasured differences in the characteristics of the groups that could explain the between-group differences observed following training.

The awareness questionnaire was specifically designed for the current study, and data about its psychometric properties were not available. Additional research on its validity and reliability is therefore necessary. The awareness scale comprised a relatively small number of items and a brief statement format may have resulted in ambiguities for carers who usually have far more comprehensive information through which to interpret behaviour. Nevertheless, the measure appeared to generate meaningful data. Indeed, the findings have been replicated by pilot studies in Austria and Greece conducted under the MEROPE project (Holt *et al*, 2000a; Tsiantis *et al*, 2004). These studies focused on the same training modules based over two-day workshops, and used translations of the awareness questionnaire.

Of course, there can be no guarantee that improved awareness scores will be translated into better practice and greater sensitivity to the mental health needs of adults with learning disabilities. Further research examining the impact of training on the ability of carers to identify potential mental health problems and to make appropriate referrals in practice is necessary. This research would help to build more complex models for understanding carer behaviour towards individuals with learning disabilities and mental health problems. Research examining the outcomes of mental health training for service users is also desirable.

Carers represent only one aspect of the recognition and referral process. Other professionals, such as GPs and social workers, also play a key role in influencing the pathway to care and it is vital that they have adequate training, especially those within generic settings. Training initiatives aimed at the broad range of professional groups providing services to individuals with learning disabilities is therefore an essential component in any strategy aimed at improving the mental health of individuals with learning disabilities.

Ultimately, training carers alone is an ineffective strategy for producing change (Clements, 1993). Without the constant reinforcement of and building on training, its effects on practice are likely to be minimal (Holt *et al*, 2000b). Training must be provided within a context of a supportive management system that provides staff with clear models in terms of first line managers acting as 'practice leaders' (Mansell *et al*, 1994; McGill & Bliss, 1993). This helps to ensure that the values developed in training are compatible with those of the organisational culture in which the individual works. Delivering training to entire teams simultaneously and tailored towards the mental health problems of the individuals they support may also be worthwhile.

Conclusion

This chapter describes the success of a brief introductory training workshop in increasing awareness of mental health problems in direct care staff working in community residential services for people with learning disabilities. Further research, incorporating randomised designs and placebo interventions, are required in order to demonstrate the impact of training on recognition and referral decisions in practice and to build more complex models of staff behaviour towards the behaviours associated with mental health problems. Training initiatives are also necessary for other groups influencing the pathway to care such as GPs, social workers and family carers. Demonstrating the outcomes of such training programmes for individuals with learning disabilities is also essential.

Acknowledgements

This project was funded by R & D London Region, Department of Health, UK. I would also like to acknowledge the invaluable contribution of Steve Hardy in providing staff training and the staff and service users who participated in the study.

References and further reading

Borthwick-Duffy SA & Eyman R K (1990) Who are the dually diagnosed? *American Journal on Mental Retardation* 98, 360–367.

Bouras N & Holt G (Eds) (1997) *Mental Health in Learning Disabilities: A Training Pack for Staff Working with People who have a Dual Diagnosis of Mental Health Needs and Learning Disabilities* (Second Edition). Brighton: Pavilion Publishing.

Clements J (1993) Some determinants of staff functioning in relation to behavioural challenges from people with learning disabilities (a view from a national training and consultancy service). In: C Kiernan (Ed) *Research to Practice? Implications of Research on the Challenging Behaviour of People with Learning Disability*. Kidderminster: British Institute of Learning Disabilities.

Edelstein TM & Glenwick S (1997) Referral reasons for psychological services for adults with mental retardation. *Research in Developmental Disabilities* 18, 45–59.

Edelstein TM & Glenwick S (2001) Direct-Care Workers' Attributions of Psychopathology in Adults with Mental Retardation. *Mental Retardation* 39, 368–378.

Emerson E & Emerson C (1987) Barriers to the effective implementation of habilitative behavioural programs in an institutional setting. *Mental Retardation* 25 101–106.

Emerson E, Moss S & Kiernan C (1999) The relationship between challenging behaviour and psychiatric disorders in people with severe intellectual disabilities. In: N Bouras (Ed) *Psychiatric and Behavioural Disorders in Mental Retardation*. Cambridge: Cambridge University Press.

Hastings R & Remington B (1994) Staff behaviour and its implications for people with learning disabilities and challenging behaviours. *British Journal of Clinical Psychology* 33, 423–38.

Holt G & Bouras N (1997) *Making Links*. Brighton: Pavilion Publishing.

Holt G, Costello H, Bouras N, Diareme S, Hillery J, Moss S, Rodríguez-Blázquez C, Salvador L, Tsiantis J, Weber G & Dimitrakaki C (2000a) BIOMED: MEROPE project: Service Provision for Adults with Mental Retardation: A European Comparison. *Journal of Intellectual Disability Research* **44** (6) 685–698.

Holt G, Costello H & Oliver B (2000b) Training Direct Care Staff About The Mental Health Needs And Related Issues of People With Developmental Disabilities. *Mental Health Aspects in Developmental Disabilities* **3** (4) 132–140.

Mansell J, Hughes H & McGill P (1994) Maintaining local residential placements. In: E Emerson, P McGill and J Mansell (Eds) *Severe Learning Disabilities and Challenging Behaviours.* London: Chapman and Hall.

McGill P & Bliss E (1993) Training clinical practitioners. In: C Kiernan (Ed) *Research to Practice? Implications of Research on the Challenging Behaviour of People with Learning Disability.* Kidderminster: British Institute of Learning Disabilities.

Moss S (2000) Psychiatric disorders in people with mental retardation. In: L Gidden (Ed) *International Review of Research in Mental Retardation.* San Diego: Academic Press.

Moss S & Patel P (1993) Prevalence of mental illness in people with learning disability over 50 years of age and the diagnostic importance of information from carers. *Irish Journal of Psychology* 14, 110–129.

Piachaud J (1999) Issues for Mental Health in Learning Disability Services. *Tizard Learning Disability Review* **4** (2) 47–48.

Quigley A, Murray GC, McKenzie K & Elliot G (2001) Staff knowledge about symptoms of mental health problems in people with learning disabilities. *Journal of Learning Disabilities* 5, 235–244.

Reiss S (1993) Assessment of psychopathology in persons with mental retardation. In: JL Matson and RP Barrett (Eds) *Psychopathology in the mentally retarded* (Second Edition). Needham Heights, MA: Allyn & Bacon.

Rojahn J, Borthwick-Duffy SA & Jacobson JW (1993) The association between psychiatric diagnoses and severe behaviour problems in mental retardation. *Annals of Clinical Psychiatry* 5, 163–70.

Spengler PM, Strohmer DC & Prout HT (1990) Testing the robustness of diagnostic overshadowing. *American Journal on Mental Retardation* 95, 204–214.

Tsiantis J, Diareme S, Dimitrakaki C, Kolaitis G, Flios A, Christogiorgos S, Weber G, Salvador-Carulla L, Hillery J & Costello H (2004) Care staff awareness training on mental health needs of adults with learning disabilities: Results from a Greek sample. *Journal of Learning Disabilities* **8** (3) 221–234.

Walshe D, O'Kelly M, Ramsay L & Gibson T (1993) The relationship between behaviour disturbance and psychiatric diagnosis in male mentally handicapped adults resident in a long term stay unit. *Irish Journal of Psychological Medicine* 10, 16–19.

Woods P & Cullen C (1983) Determinants of staff behaviour in long term care. *Behavioural Psychotherapy* 11, 4–17.

Glossary of mental health terminology

COMPILED BY ROBERT WINTERHALDER AND PETER WOODWARD

Acute	Of sudden onset, and often short in duration.
Adaptive behaviour	Implies that an advantageous change has taken place regarding behaviour.
Aetiology	The study of the causes of disease.
Alzheimer's disease	A progressive irreversible dementia of unknown origin (although research has shown a strong genetic component).
Anxiety disorder	A group of disorders such as panic disorder, generalised anxiety disorder and phobias. Characterised by unpleasant physiological (increased heart rate, rapid breathing, sweating, restlessness) and psychological (feelings of apprehension, worry, dread, fear, alertness) symptoms. This may be in response to an imagined danger.
Autism	A condition which usually manifests itself before the age of three, characterised by delay and deviation in the development of social relationships, verbal and non–verbal communication and imaginative activity, and a very restricted range of activities and interests.
Bipolar affective Disorder (manic depression)	A disorder of mood, which involves episodes of depression and mania: **depression** – the prevailing mood is one of sadness, varying from mild despondency to despair

mania – the prevailing mood is one of elation, with high spirits, excitement and over-confidence. Some individuals can become very irritable.

In both depression and mania, there are associated changes in thinking, behaviour, efficiency and physiological functioning. In very severe cases, the client may lose touch with reality, ie develop hallucinations or delusions.

Chronic	Usually refers to disorders of long duration; for example, in chronic schizophrenia it means an episode that has been continuous for two years or more.
Clouding of consciousness	A reduced awareness or misinterpretation of the surrounding environment. The individual may display poor attention and disjointed thinking.
Cognitive impairment	A decline in the level of intellectual functioning – memory, concentration, communication, orientation, general intelligence and so on.
Delirium	A condition of extreme mental and usually motor excitement, caused by a variety of physical illnesses. Delirium is marked by impaired consciousness, confusion and memory impairment, and is often accompanied by abnormal perceptions, such as hallucinations.
Delusion	A false belief, not amenable to persuasion or argument, and out of keeping with the client's cultural and educational background.
Dementia	An acquired global impairment of intelligence, memory and personality without any impairment of consciousness. Most cases are progressive and irreversible.
Depersonalisation	A change of self-awareness, such that the person feels unreal. It is an unpleasant experience.

Depression	A mental disorder characterised by a persistent lowering of mood and accompanied by various associated symptoms, such as alteration in sleep pattern, low self-esteem, diminished drive and so on.
Derealisation	An unpleasant feeling that the surrounding environment has changed and become 'unreal' or artificial. The individual feels detached and apart from their surroundings.
Environmental causes	Causes that are external, ie in the environment.
Epidemiology	The study of the prevalence and spread of disease in a community.
Flight of ideas	The person's thoughts and speech jump from one topic to other, often related but separate, topics. This may be displayed as an almost continuous flow of speech.
Genetic causes	Causes which are a result of the influence of genes. A gene contains information which codes an individual's make-up and is passed on from generation to generation.
Hallucinations	A perception in the absence of a stimulus; for example, hearing a voice when there is no sound. Hearing a voice = perception No sound = absent stimulus Hallucinations can occur in different forms; for example, visual, auditory, or to do with taste, smell or touch.
Hyperactivity	General restlessness and excessive movement.
Hypochondria	Over-concern and preoccupation about how the body functions, with an exaggeration of the symptoms of physical illnesses. The individual may fear or believe that they are unwell even when there is no evidence to suggest that they are.

Hypomania	A less severe form of mania. There is mild elevation in mood with increased energy and activity, without the hallucinations and delusions that might be seen in mania. The behaviours displayed due to hypomania are unlikely to disrupt the individual's work and social life to the extent that is seen in mania.
Hypothyroid	Diminished production of thyroid hormones from the thyroid gland in the neck. This leads to an intolerance of cold, increased weight, constipation, slow pulse, a general slowing down in all physical and mental processes, and various psychiatric manifestations such as delirium, dementia, depression or psychosis.
Illusions	A false perception to a stimuli. For example, seeing something that is there but misinterpreting it as something else. This may be more likely to happen when an individual is tired or in a room that is badly lit.
Incidence	The number of new cases of a disease in a population over a period of time.
Maladaptive	Often refers to types of behaviour that have been learned and which are inappropriate responses to the situation in question. Usually, someone suffers as a result.
Mania	Elevated or euphoric mood with increased motor activity. An individual may appear as restless or agitated and might have grandiose ideas. Other symptoms such as increased appetite, reduced sleep or flight of ideas are common. In severe cases the individual may display psychotic features with delusions reflecting the individual's grandiose mood.
Mental health problems	See **psychiatric disorders**
Mental health	The absence of a mental or behavioural disorder; mental health is a state of psychological well being in which the individual has been able to

integrate his or her more primitive drives with the norms expected by society.

Obsessive compulsive	Obsessions refer to words, ideas, images and the like, recognised by the client as his or her own, that intrude forcibly into the mind. Obsessions are unpleasant, and often the client will try to resist them. Compulsions refer to repetitive, purposeful, intentional behaviours performed in response to an obsession, such as hand washing or checking.
Organic	Physical or structural, ie not psychological or social.
Paranoid	A morbid and distorted view of the relationships between oneself and other people. Consequently, people who are paranoid are often suspicious.
Personality disorders	Disorders arising in childhood or adolescence that continue through adult life. Characterised by inflexible personalities that make it difficult for people to conform to what society considers normal, due to their maladaptive behaviour. Their behaviour often brings them into conflict with others. They are insensitive to the feelings of others and have difficulty understanding that their behaviour has an impact on others. They do not learn from their experiences, even if their previous experiences were unpleasant or harmful to themselves or others. They may appear irresponsible or demanding. Their own behaviour causes them distress.
Phobia	An irrational abnormal fear in relation to a thing, situation or stimulus which normally would not evoke such fear. The individual realises that the fear is irrational; however, the phobia often leads to avoidance of the feared stimulus or situation.

Pressure of speech/thought	The rapid appearance of varied and plentiful thoughts in an individual's mind. The individual may feel that these thoughts have been inserted into their mind by others.
Prevalence	The number of cases of a disease existing in a given population at a specific time.
Psychomotor	Refers to a combination of mental and behavioural events. For example: **psychomotor retardation** – often seen in depression, where both mental processes and the body movements are slowed down **psychomotor epilepsy** – an old term, which describes a type of epilepsy with both behavioural and mental features.
Psychopathic disorder	A type of personality disorder in which there is a deeply ingrained, maladaptive pattern of behaviour, recognisable by adolescence and continuing throughout most of adult life. The individual or society suffers. Psychopathic disorder is not a result of learning disabilities, psychosis, neurosis or any other form of psychiatric illness. The characteristics of this disorder are: self-centredness with little or no regard for the rights of others (immediate satisfaction of desire is imperative, the individual acting violently if frustrated) and associated with lack of conscience or guilt; and inability to learn from previous experience.
Psychiatric disorder	A significant behavioural or psychological pattern occurring in a person that is associated with distress, disability (an impairment in one or more areas of functioning) or with a significant risk of suffering death, pain, disability or important loss of freedom. It does not encompass an expected response to a particular event – such as the loss of a loved one – nor does it include religious, sexual or political deviant behaviours.

Mental Health in Learning Disabilities **A reader** © Pavilion Publishing (Brighton) Ltd 2005

Psychoses	A group of mental disorders characterised by an inability to recognise reality and to distinguish it from subjective experience. It is often accompanied by lack of insight (an awareness of one's own mental condition). As a result, hallucinations, delusions and so on may occur.
Schizophrenia	A group of psychiatric disorders characterised by disordered thought processes, hallucinations, delusions (false beliefs not amenable to persuasion or argument and out of keeping with the client's cultural and educational background), bizarre behaviour and social withdrawal. Not all of these characteristics have to be present to make the diagnosis.
Social	Pertaining to society; often refers to the influence of society.
Stereotypies	Repetitive primitive and self-stimulatory movements such as body–rocking and head-shaking.
Stress	Refers to factors (called stressors) which tax individuals' coping mechanisms to their limits and which, if long or severe enough, can lead to disorganised behaviour, dysfunction or disease. Examples include: **physical stressors** such as infection **psychological stressors** such as bereavement **social stressors** such as homelessness.
Vulnerability	A susceptibility to suffering, loss, disease and so on.

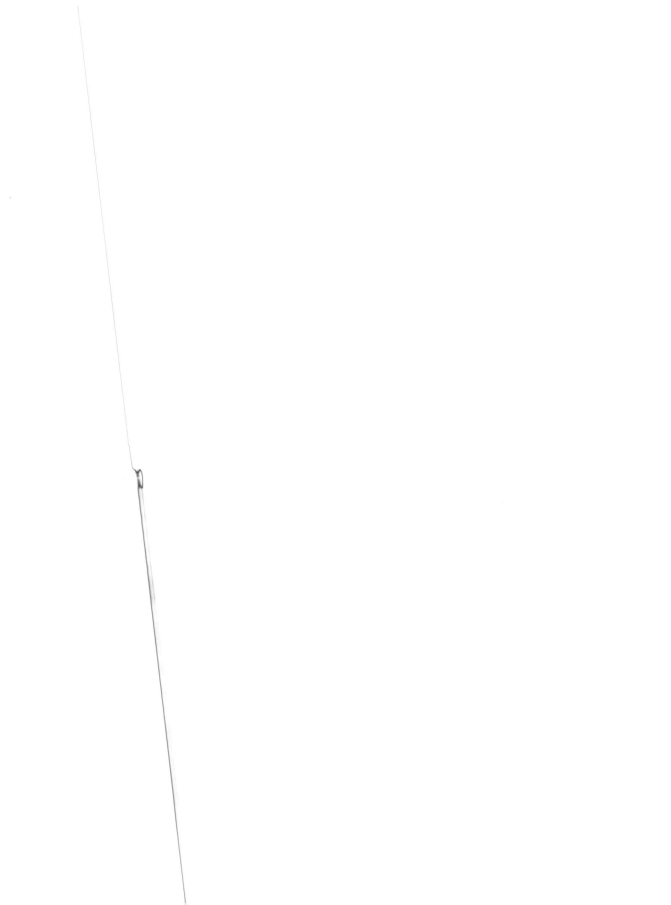

Also available from Pavilion

The Mini PAS-ADD Interview Pack

Psychiatric assessment schedules for adults with developmental disabilities

Steve Moss in association with the Estia Centre

The Mini PAS-ADD system is a set of assessment tools for undertaking mental health assessments with people with learning disabilities. It is designed to provide a smooth, reliable flow of information on psychiatric symptoms from all those involved in an individual's care, including family members, support staff and care staff.

The materials come in three parts:

- the Mini PAS-ADD handbook, for use by professionals involved in mental health assessments (comprises a semi-structured interview and clinical glossary, plus new outline training plan and coding exercises)

- packs of 20 Mini PAS-ADD interview score forms for recording the mini PAS-ADD interview scores

- packs of the Mini PAS-ADD checklist, a questionnaire written in everyday language for use by care staff and families to identify potential mental health problems and to help decide whether a further assessment is needed.

Of particular interest to: all professionals involved in mental health assessments of people with learning disabilities.

Format: handbook (94pp), 20 checklists and 20 interview score forms

Complete interview pack
Order Code: 21J   ISBN: 1 84196 073 X

Checklists only (pack of 20)
Order Code: 20J   ISBN: 1 84196 076 4

Interview score forms only★ (pack of 20)
Order Code: 19J   ISBN: 1 84196 077 2

★Please note that the score forms must be used in conjunction with the clinical glossary in the handbook

In the Know

Implementing good practice – Information and tools for anyone supporting people with a learning disability and dementia

Diana Kerr and Heather Wilkinson

This invaluable resource has been developed to help anyone who is supporting a person with learning difficulties who develops dementia. The pack contains easily accessible, straightforward, practical and realistic guidance to provide good quality care. It is arranged in three sections: background, fact sheets and tools. Each section is designed to be used alone or together with other parts of the pack.

This pack is the result of many years of research and practice by a multidisciplinary group of academic researchers, trainers and practitioners who have worked with people with learning difficulties who develop dementia, and their family and friends.

Of particular interest to: direct care staff, carers and other practitioners in the care field.

Format: ringbound resource (76pp)

Order Code: AG8   ISBN: 1 84196 166 3

Positive Goals

Interventions for people with learning disabilities whose behaviour challenges

Peter Fox and Eric Emerson

Written by eminent professionals in the field, *Positive Goals* is a resource pack which aims to help carers and professionals to identify meaningful, appropriate and socially valid interventions for people with learning disabilities whose behaviour challenges. It also provides the means to evaluate the interventions by measuring outcomes against agreed goals.

The tool is consistent with the principles of person–centred planning and facilitates an inclusive approach by ensuring that all relevant stakeholders have a say in the person's support or intervention plan.

The material provides:

- guidelines to facilitate the selection of relevant outcomes for each individual

- suggestions for collecting data appropriate to selected outcomes

- a format which enables easy adaptation for individual interventions

- background and contextual information

- guidance on preparation and a detailed case example illustrating how to use the tool.

Of particular interest to: professional staff working with people with a learning disability and challenging behaviour, including clinical psychologists, behaviour therapists, community learning disability nurses, psychiatrists, social workers, care managers and members of challenging behaviour teams.

Format: ringbound resource (70pp)

Order Code: AA1   ISBN: 1 84196 105 1

Epilepsy and Learning Disabilities

A training pack to aid teaching on epilepsy and its management

Mary Codling, Nicky MacDonald, Fiona Simpson and Barbara Chandler, Berkshire Healthcare NHS Trust

This pack provides trainers with the material to deliver training to care and residential staff on epilepsy and its management, particularly relating to epilepsy in people with learning disabilities. The pack's flexibility allows it to be used by a wide range of organisations.

The training is presented in two sessions:

- Session A: Introduction to epilepsy

- Session B: Administration of rectal diazepam (because this is an invasive medical procedure, Session B must be taught by a qualified nurse).

The pack offers step-by-step instructions, all the training materials needed to deliver the training, and two videos, The Right Stuff: facts and first aid for epilepsy and Rectal Diazepam.

Of particular interest to: residential care homes, education facilities, NHS establishments, social services, nurses, independent sector and local authorities.

Format: ringbound resource (approx 134pp) and two videos (25 mins and 20 mins)

Order Code: AF4   ISBN: 1 84196 129 9

Crossing the Minefield

Establishing safe passage through the sensory chaos of autistic spectrum disorder

Phoebe Caldwell

Building on the approach and using examples from her own extensive work in this field, Phoebe Caldwell describes how we can find ways to mark out a safe and meaningful progression from the isolation and sensory chaos experienced by people with autistic spectrum disorder to communication, relationship and a better understanding of their needs.

Of particular interest to: direct care staff, nurses, psychologists and others involved in the lives of people with learning disabilities.

Format: A4 handbook (70pp)

Order Code: AD8   ISBN: 1 84196 123 X

Person to Person

Establishing contact and communication with people with profound learning disabilities and those whose behaviour may be challenging

Phoebe Caldwell with Pene Stevens

This handbook emphasises the importance of developing a two-way relationship with individuals who have profound disabilities, whether they are autistic or whether their present behaviour is experienced as challenging.

Of particular interest to: staff who wish to become more proactive in enhancing the lives of people with learning disabilities by using their own language or familiar stimuli.

Format: A4 handbook (90pp)

Order Code: 31P   ISBN: 1 900600 43 9

You don't know what it's like

Finding ways of building relationships with people with severe learning disabilities, autistic spectrum disorder and other impairments

Phoebe Caldwell

Drawing upon her extensive experience, Phoebe Caldwell illustrates methods of communication and helps readers and staff to set aside their own sense of what 'reality' is and enables them to enter the worlds of those who are struggling to interpret and respond to sets of sensory perceptions different to those we experience in our 'normal' world. The key approach in this book is to work creatively, based on an understanding of what a person is experiencing and what it is their behaviour is trying to tell us. The text raises questions about what messages an individual is getting from the world they live in and which of these has meaning for them.

Of particular interest to: all carers working with people with autistic spectrum disorder and behavioural challenges.

Format: A4 handbook (118pp)

Order Code: 64P   ISBN: 1 84196 023 3

To order any of the above titles call our customer service team on: 0870 890 1080 (outside UK +44 (0)1273 623222, or order online: www.pavpub.com